Praise for Four Days with Dr. Deming

The book will provide us all with a living testimony to the power of Dr. Deming on stage during his four-day seminars. It will preserve the memory of those great occasions.

Dr. Michael E. Quigley
Dean, Graduate Studies
Rivier College

I know of no other book that recreates the feeling of attending one of Dr. Deming's seminars. This book captures Deming's clarity and style, which I treasure. If you ever attended Dr. Deming's seminar, this book will be a wonderful reminder of that experience. If you have never seen Dr. Deming in person, this book provides the next best thing.

Lou Cohen
Senior Consultant, Applied Marketing Science, Inc.
Author of *Quality Function Deployment: How to Make QFD Work*

This is a wonderful format for presenting Dr. Deming's theories. It will help instructors great materials and help ensure they are presenting Dr. Deming's theories accurately. I can't think of a better resource in that regard.

Maury Cotter
Director, Office of Quality Improvement
University of Wisconsin-Madison
Co-Author of *Real People Real Work* and *Kidgets: and Other Stories About Quality in Education*

Dr. Deming had much to teach us about quality, about the nature of work, and about ourselves. His four-day seminar was the vehicle by which he best expressed his philosophy. Bill Latzko and Dave Saunders have done an extraordinary job capturing the spirit of these seminars on paper. I attended many of them over the years as a facilitator, and I hear his words on these pages: An extremely valuable resource for self-study and for the classroom.

Linda M. Doherty
Director, Total Quality Leadership Office
Department of the Navy

with Dr. Deming

ENGINEERING PROCESS IMPROVEMENT SERIES

John W. Wesner, Ph.D., P.E., Consulting Editor

James H. Brill/Jerome G. Lake, *World-Class Systems Engineering*

Lou Cohen, *Quality Function Deployment: How to Make QFD Work for You*

William Fowlkes/C. M. Creveling, *Engineering Methods for Robust Product Design: Using Taguchi Methods® in Technology and Product Development*

Maureen S. Heaphy/Gregory F. Gruska, *The Malcolm Baldrige National Quality Award: A Yardstick for Quality Growth*

Jeanenne LaMarsh, *Changing the Way We Change: Gaining Control of Major Operational Change*

William J. Latzko/David M. Saunders, *Four Days with Dr. Deming: A Strategy for Modern Methods of Management*

Rohit Ramaswamy, *Design and Management of Service Processes*

Richard C. Randall, *Randall's Practical Guide to ISO 9000: Implementation, Certification, and Beyond*

John W. Wesner/Jeffrey M. Hiatt/David C. Trimble, *Winning with Quality: Applying Quality Principles in Product Development*

FOUR DAYS

with Dr. Deming

A Strategy for Modern Methods of Management

William J. Latzko and

David M. Saunders

Addison-Wesley Publishing Company

Reading, Massachusetts Menlo Park, California New York
Don Mills, Ontario Wokingham, England Amsterdam Bonn
Sydney Singapore Tokyo Madrid San Juan
Paris Seoul Milan Mexico City Taipei

The publisher offers discounts on this book when ordered in quantity for special sales. For more information please contact:

Corporate & Professional Publishing Group
Addison-Wesley Publishing Company
One Jacob Way
Reading, Massachusetts 01867

Library of Congress Cataloging-in-Publication Data
Latzko, William J., 1928–
    Four days with Dr. Deming : a strategy for modern methods of management / William J. Latzko and David M. Saunders.
        p.   cm. -- (Engineering process improvement series)
    Includes bibliographical references and index.
    ISBN 0-201-63366-3 (acid-free paper)
    1. Total quality management.   I. Deming, W. Edwards (William Edwards), 1900-   .   II. Saunders, David M.   III. Title.
IV. Series.
HD62. 15.L38 1995
658.5'62--dc20   94-29252
                                                                              CIP

ISBN 0-201-63366-3

Text printed on recycled and acid-free paper.
1 2 3 4 5 6 7 8 9 10 - CRS - 98979695
First printing January 1995

Engineering Process Improvement Series

Consulting Editor, John Wesner, Ph.D., P.E.

Global competitiveness is of paramount concern to the engineering community worldwide. As customers demand ever-higher levels of quality in their products and services, engineers must keep pace by continually improving their processes. For decades, American business and industry have focused their quality efforts on their end products rather than on the processes used in the day-to-day operations that create these products and services. Experts across the country now agree that focusing on continuous improvements of the core business and engineering processes within an organization will lead to the most meaningful, long-term improvements and production of the highest-quality products.

Whether your title is researcher, designer, developer, manufacturer, quality or business manager, process engineer, student, or coach, you are responsible for finding innovative, practical ways to improve your processes and products in order to be successful and remain world-class competitive. The **Engineering Process Improvement Series** takes you beyond the ideas and theories, focusing in on the practical information you can apply to your job for both short-term and long-term results. These publications offer current tools and methods and useful how-to advice. This advice comes from the top names in the field; each book is both written and reviewed by the leaders themselves, and each book has earned the stamp of approval of the series consulting editor, John W. Wesner.

Key innovations by industry leaders in process improvement include work in benchmarking, concurrent engineering, robust design, customer-to-customer cycles, process management, and engineering design. Books in this series will discuss these vital issues in ways that help engineers of all levels of experience become more productive and increase quality significantly.

All of the books in the series share a unique graphic cover design. Viewing the graphic blocks descending, you see random pieces coming together to build a solid structure, signifying the ongoing effort to improve processes and produce quality products most satisfying to the customer. If you view the graphic blocks moving upward, you see them breaking through barriers—just as engineers and companies today must break through traditional, defining roles to operate more effectively with concurrent systems. Our mission for this series is to provide the tools, methods, and practical examples to help you hurdle the obstacles, so that you can perform simultaneous engineering and be successful at process and product improvement.

The series is divided into three categories:

Process management and improvement This includes books that take larger views of the field, including major processes and the end-to-end process for new product development.

Improving Functional Processes These are the specific functional processes that are combined to form the more inclusive processes covered in the first category.

Special process topics and tools These are methods and techniques that are used in support of improving the various processes covered in the first two categories.

About the Authors

William J. Latzko is President of Latzko Associates, a management consulting firm specializing in quality management. He also teaches at the Fordham University Graduate School of Business. He has more than 40 years of practical experience in manufacturing and service industries, and has served as Director of Quality Control for Mundet Cork Corporation, Director of Management Science and Quality Control for CBS's Columbia Record Club, and Vice President for Quality Control for the Irving Trust Company. Formerly he was Plant Manager for the Joseph Dixon Crucible Company for Alpha Metals.

Mr. Latzko is a graduate of Fordham University and received an MBA from Rutgers University, as well as a DB from Rutgers/Stonier Graduate School of Banking. In addition, he studied statistics under Dr. Deming at New York University. He is associated with a number of professional organizations. A Fellow and Certified Quality Engineer (COE) of the American Society for Quality Control (ASQC), he is past Chairman of the Quality Management Division of the ASQC. He is also a member of the American Statistical Association and past Chairman of their Service and Support Committee. Mr. Latzko is also a widely recognized lecturer for many professional societies, including the ASQC, the ABA, and the BAI.

Mr. Latzko received the Ellis R. Ott Award for joining quality technology and management. He is the author of *Quality and Productivity for Banking and Financial Managers*, and co-author of *MICR Quality Control Handbook*. In addition, he contributed to Dr. Deming's books *Out of the Crisis*, *Quality*, and *Productivity and Competitive Position*, and has written more than 30 articles on quality control.

David M. Saunders is a Vice President at ARBOR, Inc., a firm that provides consultation, training, and research for companies and government agencies on how to achieve better quality at lower costs through customer-driven continuous improvement. A pioneer in Japanese-style hands-on customer research, Mr. Saunders has trained hundreds of workers—from Fortune 500 executives to managers and employees at all levels—in the use of these innovative quality improvement tools.

Mr. Saunders is a graduate of Hobart College and completed his graduate work at Pratt Institute and New York University with a Masters of Science. He has also completed the Fellows program in organization and community change at Johns Hopkins University.

Since entering the field in 1979, Mr. Saunders has become an acknowledged expert in using the voice of the customer to drive quality improvement. He has been a guest speaker for the ASQC, AOP, ASTD, GOAL/QPC, and the World Quality Congress. He has published numerous articles on the voice of the customer, as well as collaborating on the book *Quality and Productivity for Bankers and Financial Managers*.

Contents

Contents

Foreword by Dr. Deming

The authors of this book describe in their own words, in an interesting format, a summary of a large portion of the content of my lectures, which, I may interject, are intended to guide chief executives and stockholders, and in fact anyone that is interested in the future of American business. The style of this book is, in my opinion, commendable. I surmise that many people who find my lectures to be dull, blunt, or even depressing, will turn the pages of this book in eagerness to see what comes next.

This book makes no attempt to carry the reader into personal transformation. Personal transformation requires deep understanding of the theory of a system. It requires acceptance of the philosophy of win, win in negotiation between people, between countries, between companies, between supplier and customer, between union and management. This personal transformation is discontinuous, sudden. Once transformed, one may thereupon work toward transformation of his own organization.

It is a pleasure to commend this book to anyone for easy reading of the principles of management that must be adopted for the survival of American industry.

W. Edwards Deming
Washington
19 July 1993

Preface

We conceived the idea for this book when we met at the Toronto Annual Quality Conference. We decided then to write a book about Dr. Deming's message. The book was to be simple to read yet introduce his philosophy in a completely accurate way. We planned to use copious illustrations to make the ideas clearer.

The purpose was to make the message easy to understand. We visualized an executive, flying home after a busy day, who wanted to use the time to study a new theory without undue strain.

Would Dr. Deming like the idea? We began to work on a manuscript and laid out the first chapter with an outline. This we gave to Dr. Deming. He sent this material back, edited and with a letter: "Your idea of a book is exciting. Please continue to work on it, and get it out."

Dr. Deming not only encouraged us but actively reviewed the manuscript and added his ideas. We believe this book represents the most simple, up-to-date, and accurate presentation of his philosophy.

This book is an ideal introduction to the Deming Management Theory. Its organization follows the four-day seminar made famous by Dr. Deming. Over the course of writing the book, Dr. Deming changed the order of presentation and of emphasis. In an early draft we included a table showing the order of a presentation he made only a week before. He wrote on this table, "We have to rethink this." Subsequently he adopted the format we now follow in this book. We like to think that we have had some influence on his presentation.

The book is an ideal study tool. Undergraduate and graduate courses of Management, Organizational Development, and Quality will benefit by using this book. The material of the seminar is presented in 13 chapters—an ideal content for a semester course. The list of questions at the end of the book is useful for studying and exploring the subject matter in depth.

While this book makes a useful text for university courses, it also fills a need as a study tool for in-house training. With appropriate changes in presentation, an instructor can use this book to train all levels of management and workers. The presentation avoids as much as possible the need for any technical knowledge. The authors are working on an instructional guide for in-house training.

Those who have attended Dr. Deming's seminars in the past will find the book to be a refresher of what they experienced. It may even clarify a point that was obscure at the time of the seminar.

For those who have never attended Dr. Deming's seminar, this book gives the flavor of such an experience. To make people feel the forces at work during the seminar, we use three voices—first is Dr. Deming, who usually introduces the topic. Where we feel that we can contribute to understanding, the authors act as the second voice. An imaginary seminar participant is voice number three. The authors have much experience with the seminars, having acted often as facilitators for Dr. Deming. During this time we met many executives and managers who came to learn,

This book is the compilation of many of Dr. Deming's lectures. In attending many of these lectures, we observed his never-ending improvement—he constantly clarified his message and its delivery.

Dr. Deming's message to management is simple: The prevailing system of management is ruining us. The prevailing system focuses on short-term thinking, ranking, merit systems, management by results, quotas, and MBO's. The authors hope that by bringing Dr. Deming's message in this visual format we will help managers gain a better understanding of their jobs.

Every system, such as this book, must have an aim. Our aim is to present the Deming Seminar in a simple, enjoyable way that will give the reader understanding and desire to continue studying Dr. Deming's philosophy.

William J. Latzko
David M. Saunders
9 June 1994

impatient to get on with it but willing to listen. We have observed that changes in the seminar participant take place over time. The lesson of the beads is a particular point of change.

The epilogue was added to help people to continue to study the application of this philosophy. "There is no substitute for knowledge," said Dr. Deming. The best way to effect a transformation is with the help of a master. The authors recognize that there will be those who cannot find a master yet wish to continue studying the ideas. We give some advice that we hope will help these readers in their quest.

For a long time Dr. Deming kept saying that to manage in a competitive world requires Profound Knowledge. It was only in the last few years that he defined what he meant by Profound Knowledge. This book incorporates his most recent thinking on this important topic.

Why did we choose this format? We chose to use a nontraditional format because it is our theory that people learn in different ways. Some people are visual and can learn best when they see pictures. Others are more verbal and prefer to listen to lectures.

Traditional English text is one dimensional. A page really consists of a long line of words. (When read in one direction—left to right—this page is actually a 10-foot line of words.) Research suggests that the human brain converts information like a holograph, in three dimensions. For that reason, TVs, movies, and exhibits are popular ways of learning. Therefore, we have created this book specifically for those who prefer visual learning.

We chose to present the Four-Day Seminars in the landscape (wide page) format. Dr. Deming reviewed, corrected, and added to this manuscript. He liked the landscape format and hoped that it would appeal to the reader as well. Managing to achieve quality, by its very nature, requires the ability to see relationships. We have attempted to cross-reference the relationship between ideas whenever possible.

Acknowledgments

There are a host of people who help in writing any book. This book would never have happened without them.

First and foremost, we want to thank Dr. W. Edwards Deming for his support, encouragement, and editing. More importantly, we want to thank him for his vision, his courage, and his dedication to making America work.

Dr. Deming worked with many of the innovators in the field of quality, and often referred gratefully to their contributions. Among these pioneers, Dr. Kaoru Ishikawa, Dr. Joseph Juran, Dr. Lloyd Nelson, and Dr. Genichi Taguchi are mentioned prominently in the text.

We also wish to acknowledge the following people who have directly and indirectly contributed to this work: John Allison, Harry Artinian, Nida Backaitis, Ed Baker, Michael Brassard, Rick Brocato, Nancy Brout, Lou Cohen, Craig Cunningham, Tim Davis, John Dowd, Jim Dowhin, Bob Ferguson, Harry Freind, John Gerwels, Maureen Glassman, I. J. (Toto) Grandes del Mazo, Rich Harris, Dave Hower, Brian Joiner, Bonnie Kay, Ceil Kilian, Barbara Lawton, Michael Lowenstein, Tom Lutz, Nancy Mann, Ron Moen, Marta Mooney, Henry Neave, Joyce Orsini Nilsson, Tom Nolan, Madhav S. Phadke, Michael Quigley, Gipsie Ranney, Ken Potocki, Walter Riley, Gabe Ross, Amy Saunders, Maxine Saunders, Bill Scherkenbach, Peter Scholtes, Jim Stoner, Lou Schultz, Myron Tribus, Michael Tveite, Alan Urban, Martha Uhlhorn, Frank Werner, John Wesner, Ann Weinfeld, Don Wheeler, Abe Wolf, Kosaku Yoshida, ARBOR Inc., PACE, Quality Enhancement Seminars, and the W. Edwards Deming Institute.

No book can ever be written without the help of the authors' families, and we gratefully acknowledge their support.

To our publishers, editors, and reviewers who also helped make this a reality, our grateful thanks. We are especially thankful to Editor-in-Chief John Wait. We owe much to Associate Editor Jennifer Joss' cheerful patience and encouragement, which contributed much to making this book happen. We also thank Editorial Assistant Danielle DesMarais for keeping track of us and the reviewers. We are grateful to Production Manager Marty Rabinowitz, who has the wonderful knack of overcoming production problems that seemed insuperable to us.

Prologue

Who Is Dr. Deming

In the summer of 1950 and in numerous subsequent trips to Japan, Dr. W. Edwards Deming at their request, explained to top managers and to engineers the principles of a system, and optimization of an aim. He provided Japanese management with theories and methods that prepared the road-map of Japanese economic success.

More on Dr. Deming's Background

Dr. Deming actively edited this book, including the previous section about himself. When it came to talking about himself, Dr. Deming was very modest. We take the opportunity to fill in some further details with a time-line to introduce Dr. Deming to the reader.

1900   October 14. Born William Edwards Deming, Sioux City, Iowa

1921   B.S., University of Wyoming

1924   M.S., University of Colorado

1928   Ph.D. (mathematical physics), Yale University

1927–1939   Mathematical physicist, Department of Agriculture

1938   Invited Dr. Walter Shewhart to lecture at the Department of Agriculture

1939–1946   Adviser in sampling, Bureau of the Census

1946–1993   Professor of statistics, Graduate School of Business Administration, New York University

1946–1993   Consultant in research and industry

1950, 1951, 1952, 1955, 1960, 1965, and onward Teacher and consultant to Japanese industry, through the

1950   Japanese Union of Scientists and Engineers (JUSE)

Dr. Deming's lectures in the hot summer of 1950 were recorded by a stenographer. A book was made of these lectures. The first printing of this book was 2,000 copies. These, with many reprints, sold well in Japan. JUSE offered the royalties from this book to Dr. Deming. He returned the royalties to JUSE for use in promoting quality in Japan. These royalties became the base with which the Deming Prize was funded.

1951   JUSE established the Deming Prize for Quality.

1960   Recipient of the Second Order Medal of the Sacred Treasure, from the emperor of Japan for improvement of quality and of the Japanese economy through the statistical control of quality.

1980   The Metropolitan Section of the American Society for Quality Control established the Deming Medal in the United States. Dr. Deming was the first recipient of this award.

1980   Became famous in America by appearing on NBC TV, "If Japan Can, Why Can't We?"

1981–1993   Seminars, four days, for improvement and productivity, supported by George Washington University, attended by about 20,000 people per year.

1987   National Medal of Technology from President Ronald Reagan at the White House.

1993   December 20. Dr. Deming died at home in Washington, D.C. He is survived by two daughters and many grandchildren.

For further reading we suggest the biography written by his long-time secretary, Cecelia S. Kilian, *The World of W. Edwards Deming*, Second edition, SPC Press, Inc., 5908 Toole Drive, Suite C, Knoxville, TN 37919.

Background—Japan after World War II

Before looking at Dr. Deming's Management Theory, it is useful to recount the circumstances that made his theory appealing to the Japanese.

Japan is an island about the size of California with a population, after World War II, of about 90 million people. The sparse land permits the Japanese to grow only enough food for roughly half of this population. As a result, they had to import food. To pay for this food, they tried to export consumer goods. Because the quality of the Japanese goods was so poor in the post World War II era, the Japanese experienced a strong negative balance of trade.

General MacArthur's headquarters bought many items, used by his command, from local sources. This put as many dollars as possible into the Japanese economy. Among the larger purchases was a telephone switchboard. Upon delivery and installation, the switchboard was inoperable. Seeing this as evidence of a deep-seated problem, General MacArthur sent administrators from his staff to learn what caused this poor quality.

The study team reported that the problem was Japanese management methods. These methods were "feudal" in nature. The plant manager was the "overlord"; the rest of the plant were "serfs." The Japanese used the same methods of management that America used at the turn of the century. This style suggests the management philosophy of Frederick W. Taylor.

The research team urged the formation of unions to counter the despotic management style. General MacArthur embraced this advice. Unions of all sort proliferated.

The Union of Japanese Scientists and Engineers (better known as "JUSE" from its telegraphic acronym) formed during this time. One of the first issues they faced was that of the growing negative balance of trade. It was plain that bad quality was the problem. To sell in overseas markets, Japanese products had to have improved quality. JUSE decided to get help from a master.

In the hot summer of 1950 (10–18 July), JUSE invited Dr. W. Edwards Deming to teach some 600 engineers in four Japanese cities. Dr. Deming saw trouble ahead. If he lectured solely to engineers the whole process would not last more than three years.

Based upon his experience in the United States during and after World War II, Dr. Deming knew the need for top management's involvement for the quality effort to work. At the start of the war, Dr. Deming advised that courses be held in the use of Statistical Process Control. These courses were highly effective, and they contributed to the victory.

The period after World War II saw many wartime Quality Control Departments disbanded. Management saw these units as needless costs in a consumer era.

The understanding and leadership of top management are needed to get high quality. Quality is not a function of the individual but of the system.

Dr. Deming shared his concerns with Mr. Ichiro Ishikawa. Mr. Ishikawa's solution was to send invitations to the 32 top executives in Japan. The invitation summoned them to attend a special lecture by Dr. Deming at the Tokyo Economics Club.

Dr. Deming taught Japanese executives that customers and suppliers are part of the same system. The improvement of this system must be never ending.

Dr. Deming credits Dr. Walter Shewhart with teaching him that there are two ways of doing things: the old way and the new way.

Dr. Deming Teaches in Japan

The old way is:

1. Design   2. Make   3. Sell

Depicting this attitude is Henry Ford's statement, "You can have any color car you want as long as it is black." What was the reason for choosing black? Black dries faster and because it dries faster, production is faster. Ford was slow to accept that customers liked a choice of colors. Competitors that offered a choice soon thrived.

Dr. Deming showed the Japanese the new model (new in 1929) called the Shewhart Cycle.[1] This model starts with design, goes on to making the product, selling it, and testing in service. Then it uses the test results to make improvements.

The diagram below shows this model:

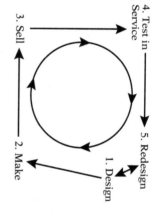

4. Test in Service

5. Redesign

1. Design

3. Sell

2. Make

Japanese top managers studied and used these concepts. They learned to manage quality. They realized the value of consumer satisfaction. They understood the necessity of finding the consumer needs. They became expert at filling these needs before consumers even realized that they existed, with quality that the customer never even realized was possible, such as automatic focus cameras.

Japanese managers realized the Shewhart Cycle is also a cycle of learning: Plan-Do-Study-Act.

An illustration is below:

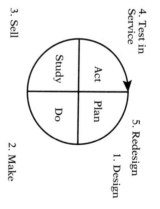

4. Test in Service

Study | Act

Plan | Do

5. Redesign

1. Design

3. Sell

2. Make

A review in detail of the cycle of learning comes later in this text.

Dr. Deming taught management theory as well as Statistical Process Control (SPC); most Americans are not aware of his many major contributions to market research and marketing. Modern research methods are fundamentally different from older research methods (e.g., Customer Window™).[2]

[1] Dr. Walter A. Shewhart is best known for his pioneering work, *Economic Control of Quality of Manufactured Product*. In his 1939 book, *Statistical Methods from the Viewpoint of Quality Control*, he discusses "... the dynamic scientific process of acquiring knowledge" (p. 45).

[2] Saunders, D.M. "Customer Window," *Quality Progress*, June, 1987.

Why Should I Read This Book

The principles taught in this lecture are new to business schools. **Some business schools are very interested in adopting these methods of management.**[3]

[3] Fordham Graduate School of Business teaches these methods of management

I went to

_____
Business School,
surely I learned
what is important.

Fill in the blank:

☐ Harvard
☐ Stanford
☐ Wharton
☐ School of
   Hard Knocks

Our guess:

☐ Some will read, understand, and act.
☐ Some will read and not understand.
☐ Others will not read —they are too busy
   stamping out brush fires.

The choice is yours!!

How to Read This Book

DR. DEMING'S VOICE: This book is based on actual lectures given by Dr. Deming from the 1980s up to one of Dr. Deming's last lectures in 1993. Dr. Deming personally corrected the manuscript to reflect his latest thinking in 1993.

During the actual lectures Dr. Deming's acerbic wit pervades. Attempts will be made to capture this humor. (Laughter) will be used to indicate audience laughter.

When we quote Dr. Deming's words we use either quotation marks (") or the font used in this paragraph.

AUTHORS' VOICE: We also explain a number of Dr. Deming's points. These explanations use the font of this paragraph.

EXECUTIVE'S VOICE: To give the feeling of reality we use a fictional executive who attends the Seminar. This executive is a composite of the many met by the authors as they assisted Dr. Deming. The executive gives examples of application throughout the text. These examples come from the real-life experience of the authors' consulting practice. They are kept anonymous. We use the italic font of this paragraph to distinguish the attending executive from Dr. Deming's and our words.

Most of the charts Dr. Deming uses in his four-day seminar are reproduced here. Additional charts are added by the authors.

Editorial comments are within a heavy box rule. These comments may also include the voice of the curious reader.

Main points are within gray boxes.

The four-day lectures start at 9:00 A.M. and run to 4:00 P.M. each day, with a one-hour lunch break and morning and afternoon coffee breaks.

At 4:00 each day Dr. Deming's helpers distribute questions to those in attendance. The people in attendance form discussion teams to answer assigned sets of questions. Their answers are recorded on index cards. Selected answers are read at the start of next morning's session. The authors, along with other Deming helpers would read the many hundreds of answers each night and list the best responses on an overhead the next morning.

Although Dr. Deming lectured for the entire four days, he interspersed his talk with questions and answers as well as short examples from Mr. Latzko and others.

William Latzko worked with Dr. Deming for over thirty years. In the past fifteen years, Dr. Deming constantly improved his lecture. This book encompasses lecture's elements including Dr. Deming's own corrections to the text late in 1993, which represents the last version given by Dr. Deming.

Overview

	Day One	Day Two	Day Three	Day Four
8:00	Registration Introduction	Working Group Responses	Working Group Responses	Working Group Responses
9:00	How are we doing?	The Management of People	Variation	Applications
	The heavy losses	The Red Beads	Examples	Training and Leadership
	System of Profound Knowledge	Shewhart and Control Charts	The Funnel	Service Organizations
	The 14 Obligations of Management		Tampering	Improvement for Living
4:00	Structured Group Discussion	Structured Group Discussion	Structured Group Discussion	
6:30				

1

The Need for Transformation of Western Management

DAY FOUR | DAY THREE | DAY TWO | DAY ONE

Dr. Deming Lectures to a Packed Convention Hall

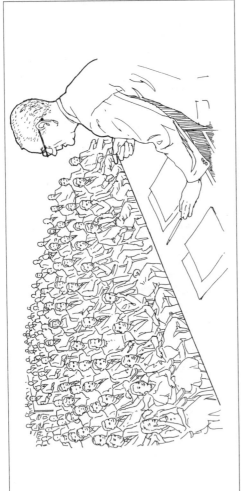

From 20 February to 23 February, 1990, Dr. Deming lectured to a packed convention hall at the Adams Mark Hotel in Philadelphia. This lecture was sponsored by the Philadelphia Chamber of Commerce, Philadelphia Area Council for Excellence (PACE).

This scene has been repeated many times throughout the world. The authors have assisted Dr. Deming at many lectures by coaching working groups, making mini-presentations and answering questions.

This book is not a substitute for attending actual lectures. Textbooks accompanying the lecture were *Out of the Crisis* and *The New Economics* by Dr. W. Edwards Deming, and *The Deming Route* by William W. Scherkenbach.

Commentary in this book is focused on materials from over a dozen recent lectures given by Dr. Deming, and we have liberally quoted from his writings.

I enter the grand ballroom. It is packed with people, mostly men. Most in dark suits, a hefty sprinkling of military uniforms, some in business casual. An old man in a blue traditional three-piece suit sits alone at the head table. He is looking over his notes. Occasionally a young woman will approach him for a short conference. Then someone from the audience will present him with a book to autograph. He seems very approachable.

The representative from the Chamber of Commerce gives a short intro and then the audience all rise in a storm of applause. Dr. Deming looks embarrassed, his face breaks into a smile, he motions for us to sit, and then he begins.

Why Are We Here

> **"Some are here out of curiosity.**
> **Some to get a day off from work.**
> **Some have no idea why they are**
> **here.**
> **But you must have an aim.**
> **Our aim is to have fun."**

"The prevailing system of management has crushed fun out of the workplace. The prevailing system of education has crushed fun out of the schools.

"How can you do that? It's very simple. Have grades in school. (Laughter) Annual appraisal for people, that will do it. (Laughter) Those things are no fun.

"We are going to learn about the prevailing system of management. How to take joy out of life.

"We have been misled. This age will go down in history as the age of mythology. We ought to be leading the world."

Why would you attend this lecture?
- ☐ My boss sent me.
- ☐ My customers told me to learn Deming or else.
- ☐ I've been reading and thinking about this for a long time.
- ☐ I'm concerned about America's future.

Historical Perspective

Dr. Deming challenges the audience to reexamine the past. He challenges our view of history, our beliefs and values, even our definition of the American Dream.

"After World War II, America had tremendous prosperity. We made fantastic profits. Goods from our factories were sold all over the world. People clamored for our goods. WHY?

"Was it because we were so brilliant, our goods of such high value? Was it because our plants were so efficiently run, our designs so clever, our marketing so on-target? Was it because our managers and workers had pride in their work?

"Some suggest postwar prosperity was due to our genius, our Yankee ingenuity. Wasn't it America's "manifest destiny" to replace the British Empire as the world's industrial and military leader? Or was it an historical accident?

"Who was our competition in the world marketplace in the early 1950s? Were there many fully functioning factories in Europe, Asia, Africa, or Latin America? How about Japan and Germany?

"Basically North America was untouched by the ravages of war. America was the only game in town when it came to manufacturing. If you wanted a tractor, train, boat, or plane you had to buy it from a North American company.

"We had the only factories that were undamaged by fighting. Our factories were intact, and at full capacity. The factories of other nations were completely destroyed.

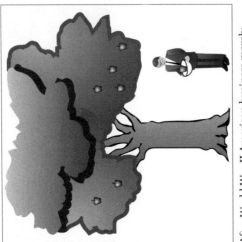

After World War II American business merely had to go to the apple tree with their baskets. The apples fell in. People throughout the world wanted American products; quality mattered little.

"With this huge industrial capacity it was simple for us to prosper. It was as if we merely had to go over to an apple tree and hold out our baskets. The apples just fell in.

"Some people still managed to go broke. It was hard to do." (Laughter)

NOTE: American management style after World War II was often the authoritarian style needed to command combat troops. Unfortunately, Americans confused an authoritarian management style with postwar boom. The baseball player who scratches his head and then hits a home run will repeat this behavior again and again, in the hope of another home run. America mistakenly thought its authoritarian management practices led to postwar prosperity. William Ouchi, in *The M-Form Society* has called this effect "superstitious learning," a way people learn that is well documented by psychologists.

Is America Prosperous or Are We in Trouble

Give your opinion below:

Are we prosperous?
Yes, because we have:

☐ a huge GNP

☐ great natural resources

☐ abundance of capital

☐ stock prices are high

☐ _____

☐ _____

☐ _____

☐ _____

☐ _____

☐ _____

Are we in trouble?
Yes, because we have:

☐ negative trade balance

☐ large government spending

☐ exhausted natural resources

☐ shaky capital market

☐ _____

☐ _____

☐ _____

☐ _____

☐ _____

☐ _____

DAY ONE

America Is in Trouble—More Is Going out Than Coming in

Dr. Deming shows this information on an overhead projector. "Our balance of trade has been on the decline for over 17 years. What will this mean to you? What will a huge trade deficit mean to your children? How will we survive the future? Does devaluing the dollar help? Will we continue to lose jobs across America?"

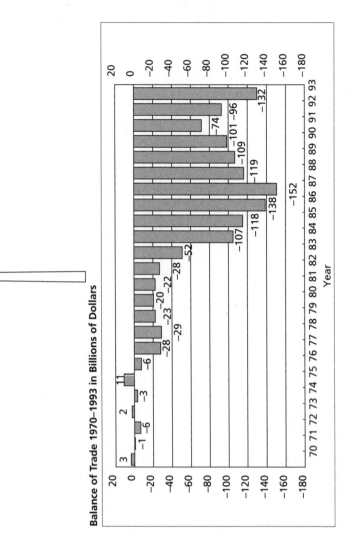

Balance of Trade 1970–1993 in Billions of Dollars

Year

Aren't We Still Leaders in Agriculture

"What about agriculture? Surely it is an American success story? Yes, in many ways agriculture is an example of doing things right."

Most in the audience are thinking that agriculture will show up as a case of America exporting to the rest of the world. Dr. Deming reminds us that if you include the cost of illicit drugs, we now import more than we export.

Even the trade balance on agriculture has declined.

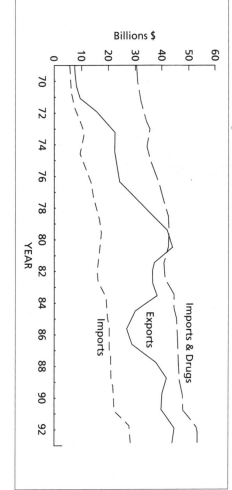

Dr. Deming adds:
"1988 drugs captured at the border:

$ 124,000 per agent
$ 3,640,000 per dog

The answer to our drug problem. Hire more dogs." (Laughter)

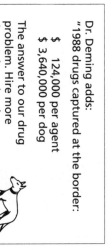

What American Industry Brings in the Most Dollars

What is your choice?

☐ agriculture
☐ raw materials
☐ manufactured goods
☐ machinery
☐ aircraft
☐ instruments
☐ scrap metals
☐ movies
☐ _____
☐ _____

Dr. Deming tells this story:

"Dr. Dana M. Cound (former president of the American Society for Quality Control) sent me a list of 99 American products, noted for being the best in the world. The list contained:

- chewing gum
- cigarettes, and
- paper clips

"Paper clips, we have the best in the world, we should be thankful." (Laughter)

Dr. Deming repeats: "What American industry brings in the most dollars?"

Audience: "Movies."

Dr. Deming: "Yes, American movies, known the world over."

Audience: "Banking."

Dr. Deming: "No. No. Now the biggest American banks are 17th on the list of international banks. What about the Savings and Loan crisis? What about bank failures? Do you call that quality? What has happened to America? Why do we need a transformation? What is our problem?"

Audience: "Unfair foreign competition."

Dr. Deming: "Well is it? People like to buy foreign products. Why do people prefer foreign products? Look at my pen. The one made overseas writes on the overhead projector every time. The one from America skips. Which would you buy? Our problem is QUALITY."

Dr. Deming once again appeals to our common sense.

"How about a national referendum:

Are you in favor of quality?

☐ Yes
☐ No

"Secret ballot. Express yourself. (Laughter)

"He who is not for quality, let him stand!" (Laughter)

What Factors Have Led to American Prosperity in the Past

"America has had vast natural resources. We had an entire continent with huge forests, rich minerals, fertile soil and a temperate climate. We had plenty of land, a ready flow of immigrants who conveniently arrived in waves that often matched industrial development.

"These natural resources have made it easy for us to develop a vast agricultural and industrial base."

Dr. Deming chides his audience, asking, "We were blessed with natural resources? Right?

"WRONG, WE HAVE BEEN CURSED WITH AN ABUNDANCE OF NATURAL RESOURCES."

What Dr. Deming means is that we have had so much in the way of resources that we have been careless in how we use them.

Just digging money out of the ground.

"The Mesabi Range in 1920 produced 74 percent iron ore. Now it contains 33 percent iron ore.

"We have sold off our natural resources. Once they are gone they are gone forever. Our oil is being used up. It is non-renewable.

"What about trade barriers? What country has the most trade barriers today?"

The audience answers: "The United States."

Dr. Deming: "The United States is correct. We don't give grades here, but you get an A. (Laughter)

"Three years ago France was number one. We were only number two. But we have caught up." (Laughter)

What Is the Definition of a Colony

A colony is a nation that sells off raw materials and buys back manufactured goods.

We began as a colony; we have become one again.

What a curious idea Dr. Deming has presented. Is it possible that America could, once again, become a colony?

Most of us believe that American wealth extends from our hard work, our individual efforts. We are a nation of entrepreneurs.

I find it repugnant to think that American success is due to historical accident or geographical luck.

Even the thought of America being anything less than number one is impossible, unthinkable.

I wonder where Dr. Deming is heading. I am sitting in a room filled with hundreds and hundreds of people like myself—business people from companies throughout the country. Could all of these companies be in trouble?

Something Has Happened to America

"At the turn of the century (1900s) one could write home to Europe and say 'come to America, work hard and prosper . . .'

"In America, everyone has his own life preserver. It's each man for himself. This damages our companies and our ability to compete in a world marketplace.

"Our prosperity has been growing for the first part of this century. But it has leveled off, we are at a turning point. We can prosper again, or continue our decline. Down the tubes. (Laughter)

"Without two-income families, how many American families would already realize the decline?"

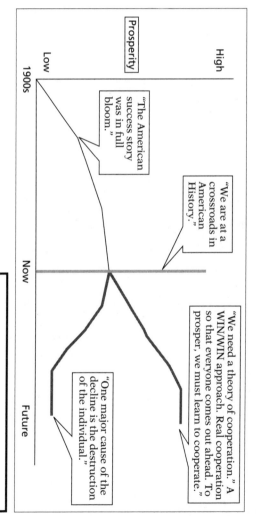

High

| Prosperity |

Low

1900s   Now   Future

"The American success story was in full bloom."

"We are at a crossroads in American History."

"We need a theory of cooperation." A WIN/WIN approach. Real cooperation so that everyone comes out ahead. To prosper, we must learn to cooperate."

"One major cause of the decline is the destruction of the individual."

Dr. Deming suggests that we manage by reflex action. We do not manage by planning. Reflex action is what a cat does when it has touched a hot stove. It reacts. It jumps. He suggests that managers throughout America merely react to a never-ending series of random events.

DAY ONE

Reflections During Coffee Break

Sure I understand that times have changed, that America is not quite what it once was, but is Dr. Deming carrying things too far? Our unemployment rate is lower than it was in the late 1970s. Sure we owe money, but so does most of the rest of the world. Also, we are doing many things to improve.

My company has an active cost-cutting program underway. We are aggressive in pushing zero defects, we are training hundreds of line workers in Quality Circles, we have a new incentive pay program in which each division competes and a profit sharing pool is then split up each year, we've got an employee of the month in each plant, and then on top of all that we have purchased this new automatic inspection equipment system that won't let a single defect through.

That's not all. As President and CEO I have delegated the task to a Director of Total Quality Management. I give him the authority and responsibility to brief me and all the vice-presidents each quarter on TQM progress.

So sure, what Dr. Deming has to say interests me, but things really aren't so alarming. I figure that we should have TQM installed in about two years.

I've heard about all the warnings, but this shouldn't be much harder than when we installed MBO. We are still waiting for the results.

I better get to a phone so that I can call the office and hear about today's brush fires.

To Achieve Quality There is No Substitute for Knowledge

As we return from coffee break Dr. Deming is tapping on the microphone.

Tap, tap, tap.

Tap, tap, tap.

"When I was in Japan, 'tap, tap, tap' was the sound made by the fire watcher on patrol tapping two sticks together. When you heard the tap, tap, tap, you knew that everything was OK.

"No one is saying that management is stupid. Not at all. They do their best. They simply lack a theory of profound knowledge to guide their decisions.

"Where are the financial people who write checks for equipment that automatically tampers with the process? **How could they know?**

"He who is not in favor of best efforts, let him stand (Laughter).

"Sure we want best efforts; but best efforts must be guided by theory and knowledge.

"Those who only give us best efforts—let them stay home, in bed, and sleep late. We would all be better off. (Laughter).

They only tamper and make things worse.

"When these approaches are used without the benefit of profound knowledge they are counter-productive."

Quick Fix—Machinery and Automation

It takes more than engineering knowledge to design and use automated equipment. It takes profound knowledge to get the proper design of the equipment.

Some large companies found that their bid to improve quality through automation has backfired. A bank worked hard to build an automated process. The process lets a corporate treasurer learn his account balances at once. It also lets him move funds based on the data. The first response to the system was enthusiastic. However, soon complaints came.

The bank responded by adding more features. The complaints increased. Finally, the whole project failed.

The problem was that the communications network could not handle the extra load of work. At critical times, the treasurers called the system but the lines were busy.

Automation and new features were not the answer. The answer was to get the existing system to work properly.

A drug firm bought a new machine to make pills. It is key to make the weight of each pill the same. The manufacturer offered an expensive device to check the pill weight. It weighs each pill and computes the difference between the real weight and the required weight. The machine adjustment is equal to this amount.

If the producer of the machine had understood Rule 2 of the Funnel Experiment (see page 152), he would never have made the device. He would have focused instead on making his equipment better.

"If you could follow me around in my consultations you would see that much automation is a source of poor quality and high cost, helping put us out of business. Much of it, if it performs as intended, is built for twice the capacity that is needed. For it is poorly designed, such as:

make inspect ◆ make inspect ◆ make inspect where inspection may not be economically the best procedure. (See page 50ff.) Moreover, the apparatus for inspection usually gives more trouble than the apparatus for manufacturing."

Quick Fix—Just In Time (JIT)

Just In Time, along with low inventory, is good, of course. Unfortunately, efforts usually start at the wrong end.

The place to start is with processes and movements of material used. Once processes and movements are in statistical control, the plant manager will know how much of this and that he will need by 3 o'clock tomorrow. Quantity and quality will be predictable.

Many companies use Just In Time (JIT) as a way to achieve quality. This puts the cart before the horse. Just In Time is possible only when the processes are under statistical control. If the material ordered under Just In Time principles has defective items, the production will suffer. To protect themselves in such a situation, local management will order extra material, a policy of Just In Case.

An example of such a policy was the decision in a major organization to deliver office supplies only once a week. In case of emergency, a special order was sent. This policy resulted in a savings of five people in the supply area. The emergency provision was far from timely. The result was that every secretary had a cache of office supplies to last out the month. Inventory for these supplies rose from $5 million to $20 million per year. The secret hoards accounted for this change.

Quick Fix—Cost Cutting

"We beat
down costs."

"Too often, the financial people in a company merely beat down costs, on the thought that any cost is too high. Why do they write checks for machinery that violates good practices?"

Big Losses are Unstudied

"Without understanding Profound Knowledge, financial people just chase nickels and dimes. Of course one should chase nickels and dimes, but it is futile to chase nickels and dimes while at the same time neglecting the biggest losses.

"Figures for the biggest losses,' as Dr. Lloyd S. Nelson said years ago, 'are unknown and unknowable.' Without Profound Knowledge, the biggest losses are not even under suspicion."

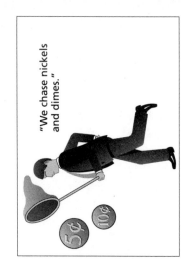

"We chase nickels
and dimes."

Quick Fix—Suboptimization of People and Technology

"It takes knowledge to optimize a given person and a given piece of machinery.

"Without Profound Knowledge we end up optimizing one part of the system, but lose out elsewhere in the system.

"One area may be greatly improved, but this can cause two other areas to decline. Without Profound Knowledge a manager would never know."

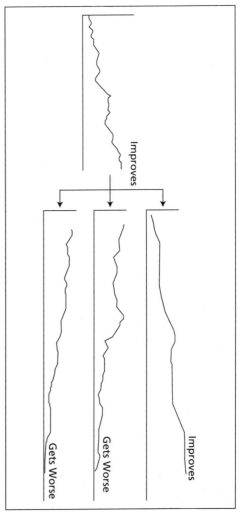

Improves

Improves

Gets Worse

Gets Worse

"One down-stream process improves, but two others get worse."

(See page 188, for example of how the purchasing department made improvements, but created known losses elsewhere.)

Quick Fix—Management by Results

**Driving by rearview mirror:
This is like looking at the past to
see where you are going in the
present and where you will be in
the future.**

Imagine that we have taped paper over
the windshield, and that to drive home
you have to rely on your rearview mirror. You could drive, but not very well.
That is like relying on feedback, on
numbers from the past. Control charts
give us a chance to predict the future.
Not perfectly, there is risk. But at least
we see what our system will probably
do in the future. Then we can plan, we
can set prices, we can predict.

Driving with the front windshield
covered we rely on side and rear mir-
rors. It makes no sense. Yet management reports for last week, last month,
and last year are looks into the past.
Control charts are predictions into the
future. Which would you prefer?

Dr. Gipsie Ranney said that to look at
costs as though they were causes is misleading. Costs are the result of causes.

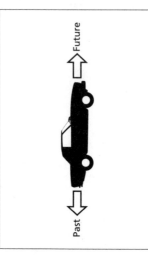

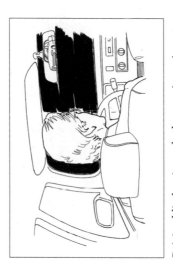

Driving blind: using only the rearview mirror to
drive forward. Hope that there are no curves.

Quality Is Made in the Boardroom—Not on the Factory Floor

> Quality of output of a company cannot be better than quality directed at the top.

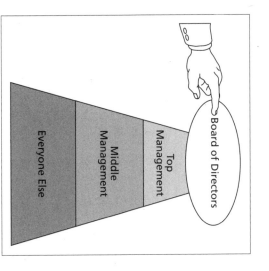

Board of Directors

Top Management

Middle Management

Everyone Else

Dr. Deming's American viewgraph pen stops writing. He says, "I think I'll use my imported pen. Which would you buy?" (Laughter)

"The president of a company (who doesn't know any better) says he has put quality in the hands of his plant managers.

"THIS IS WRONG.

"The poor plant manager:

didn't design the product,

didn't decide the marketing,

didn't decide the pricing, and

didn't pick the suppliers.

"Yet we say he is responsible for quality.

"This is wrong.

"What could be worse than the job of plant manager? Works hard as a dog, except that some dogs don't work." (laughter)

"Delegation at all levels needs to be reconsidered. When is it appropriate, when not? We in America have been taught: when in doubt, delegate."

Forces of Destruction

The prevailing system of management finds many uses. Application is found in all phases of our life, from birth on. Everyone is affected. The system is so common today that it is rarely questioned. Yet it is the root cause of our current decline.

We have become obsessed with tests and competition, all in the name of fairness. We test children as early as kindergarten. The result of these tests and grading subtly influence their performance. Peter Kapsales calls this the Pygmalion effect.[1] It becomes a self-fulfilling wish. "Bright" students advance, "dull" students do not do well.

The same effect is prevalent in the business world. Those with good appraisals do well while those with poor appraisals are best off looking for another job. They are doomed in their current position.

One hears derogatory remarks about bureaucrats. The question to ask is how they got to be so bad? Before they joined the organization they seemed to be all right. On being hired they are enthusiastic, ready to conquer the world. Yet, within a week or two they act like everyone else—poorly.

Could it be our style of management? Is it the heritage of Frederick Taylor's management philosophy?

Whatever the cause we are stuck with many shibboleths. These cannot stand rigorous, and sometimes not so rigorous, examination. Dr. Deming raises this issue. Until we change our style of management to rest on a logical basis, the evils of the current system will persist. Dr. Deming proposes solutions.

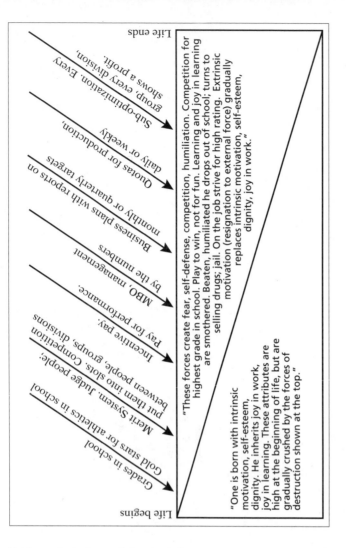

Forces of Destruction diagram. "Life begins" at bottom, "Life ends" at top, with a descending series of labels:
- Grades in school
- Gold stars for athletics in school
- Merit System. Judge People; put them into slots. Competition between people, groups, divisions
- Incentive pay. Pay for performance.
- MBO management by the numbers.
- Business plans with reports on monthly or quarterly targets
- Quotas for production, daily or weekly.
- Sub-optimization. Every group, every division, shows a profit.

"One is born with intrinsic motivation, self-esteem, dignity. He inherits joy in work, joy in learning. These attributes are high at the beginning of life, but are gradually crushed by the forces of destruction shown at the top."

"These forces create fear, self-defense, competition, humiliation. Competition for highest grade in school. Play to win, not for fun. Learning and joy in learning are smothered. Beaten, humiliated he drops out of school; turns to selling drugs; jail. On the job strive for high rating. Extrinsic motivation (resignation to external force) gradually replaces intrinsic motivation, self-esteem, dignity, joy in work."

[1]Kapsales, Peter, *The Age of Punishment*, unpub., 1991.

Story of the Art Class

Dr. Deming is right. Grades in school hurt motivation. Art interested my daughter when she was young. We sent her to a neighborhood school run by a retired teacher. My daughter would return from class each week with a smile. The teacher was full of praise and support for her art work.

Every few weeks she would come home with a project, something that we all could be proud of. A painting or a drawing that we would frame and put on the wall.

So in high school she took more art classes. She even thought of a major in art.

Then she took a class from the head of the art department. This teacher graded every drawing and painting. My daughter would come home bitter and angry. Soon she began to lose interest in art. What is a parent to do? Go to the school and meet with the principal? Meet with the teacher? I'm afraid we do the same thing at work. We grade people and then they lose interest.

You get only a C on this art project

The Prison

Dr. Deming tells us that management in the Western world has put them-selves and us into a prison.[2] A prison that is invisible, yet holding us as strong as any edifice of brick and mor-tar. Managers of the Western world are not even aware that they are in this state of captivity. "How could they know?" asks Dr. Deming.

What got us into this state? Professor Ouchi suggests a reason in his book, *The M-Form Society.*

"We enjoyed forty years of unprece-dented industrial monopoly during which our companies earned monop-oly profits, labor took home monopoly wages, and government extracted monopoly taxes. When there is such a monopoly, the stage is set for supersti-tious learning."[3]

These decades saw all sorts of theo-ries tried. Invariably, they worked. This confirmed the belief system of Western managers.

Frederick W. Taylor (1856–1915), also known as the father of scientific management, formulated many of these beliefs. Taylor made the point that a worker playing sports "... strains every nerve to secure victory for his side." He then goes on to state:

"When the same workman returns to work on the following day, instead of using every effort to turn out the largest possible amount of work, in a majority of the cases this man deliber-ately plans to do as little as he safely can—to turn out far less work than he is well able to do—in many instances to do not more than one-third to one-half of a proper day's work."[4]

The key factor in Taylor's manage-ment theory depends on the essential laziness of the worker and all but the top levels of management. From this theory evolved various incentive sys-tems and Management By Objective.

Taylor told management that they and only they were knowledgeable and trustworthy. In effect he said that work-ers should park their brains at the door. They should do exactly as they are told. Management must see that they follow orders exactly. Taylor would have been delighted with the slogan, "Do it right the first time." We will examine the fal-lacy of this slogan later.

Dr. Deming tells us that "the prevail-ing system of management, has been created by best efforts not guided by knowledge." We will examine some of the aspects of the prison and then see that Dr. Deming has a solution, the sys-tem of Profound Knowledge.

[2] The metaphor of the prison and the walls was suggested to Dr. Deming by Dr. Nida Backaitis.

[3] Ouchi, William G., *The M-Form Society,* (Addison-Wesley, 1984) p. 4.

[4] Taylor, Frederick W. *The Principles of Scientific Management,* Easton: Hive Publishing Company, 1985, p. 13.

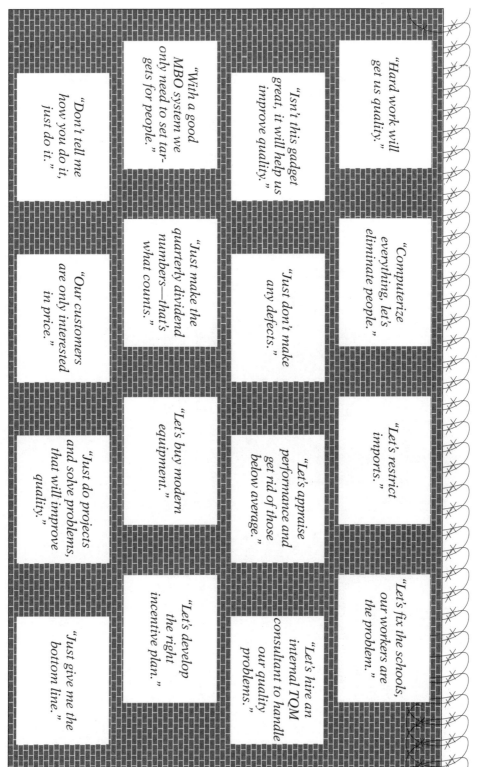

DAY ONE

Escape from Prison

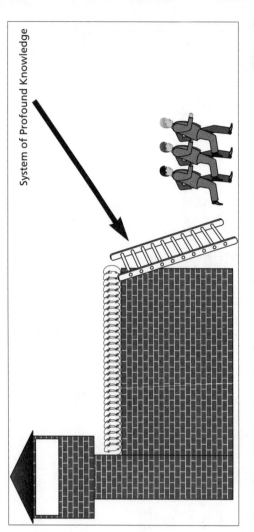

System of Profound Knowledge

The prison is the current scheme of management. In the last century a myth formed: "If you can't measure it, you can't manage it." This myth is a direct outgrowth of the laws of scientific management (Taylor, circa 1890). It has put us into the "prison."

Dr. Nelson stated, "The most important figures needed for management of any organization are unknown and unknowable."[5] The "scientific" approach neglects the vital factors that are not quantifiable. Just because it is not possible to measure the results of actions is no ground for ignoring or not managing them.

Not enough heed has been paid to the factors that caused our decline. Dr. Deming has given us a method to deal with the problems logically, a system called "Profound Knowledge."

Escape from prison requires this system of Profound Knowledge. The individual solutions (such as zero defects, JIT, SPC, Quality Circles, best efforts) won't work if they are not part of a larger system of Profound Knowledge.

[5]Dr. Lloyd S. Nelson, quoted in Dr. W. Edwards Deming's, *Out of the Crisis*, Cambridge: MIT Center for Advanced Engineering Study, 1986, p. 20.

2

A System of Profound Knowledge

DAY FOUR | DAY THREE | DAY TWO | DAY ONE

What Is a System of Profound Knowledge?

"Hard work and best efforts, put forth without guidance of profound knowledge may well be at the route of our ruination. There is no substitute for knowledge. What is profound knowledge?"[1]

- Appreciation for a system
- Theory of Variation
- Theory of Knowledge
- Understanding of Psychology

"I was just thinking about Profound Knowledge at a banquet last night at the Waldorf Astoria. I was awarded a prize for quality assurance. I haven't opened it yet! (Laughter). Can you imagine such nonsense? Quality can't be assured (after the fact), it must be built in.

"I stayed in the Waldorf before. I knew a man that stayed there regularly. He was going broke. I guess he stayed there to enjoy the ride down the tube." (Laughter)

How do you prevent doing the wrong thing? The system of *Profound Knowledge* is a framework for applying best efforts to the right tasks. It treats processes from a system's slant using statistical principles. The theory of knowledge is utilized for prediction. A knowledge of psychology is needed because we deal with people.

"The various segments of Profound Knowledge cannot be separated. They interact with each other. Thus, knowledge of psychology is incomplete without knowledge of variation.

"One need not be eminent in any part of Profound Knowledge in order to understand it as a system, and to apply it."

[1] Dr. W. Edwards Deming, *Foundation for Management of Quality in the Western World*, a paper delivered at a meeting of The Institute of Management Sciences in Osaka, 24 July 1989, updated 1 September 1990, p. 11. Dr. Deming's Theorem 2 is, "We are being ruined by best efforts."

What Is a System

"A system is a series of functions or activities (subprocesses, stages—hereafter components) within an organization that work together for the aim of the organization.[2]

"The components are necessary but not sufficient to accomplish the aim of the system. There is in almost any system interdependence between the components thereof. The greater the interdependence between components, the greater the need for communication and cooperation between them.

"The aim, the values and beliefs of the organization, as set forth by top management, are important. The aim of the system must be clear to everyone in the system. Without an aim, there is no system. The performance of any component is to be judged in terms of its contribution to the aim of the system, not for its individual production or profit, nor for any other competitive measures.

"If the aim, size, or boundary of the organization changes, then the functions of the subcomponents will change for optimization of the new system. Management of a system, therefore, requires knowledge of the interrelationship between all the subprocesses within the system and of everybody that works in it.

"Management's job is to optimize the entire system. Suboptimization is costly. It would be poor management, for example, to optimize sales, or to optimize manufacture, design of product, or of service, or incoming supplies, to the exclusion of the effect on other stages of production (suboptimization)."

[2] Deming, W. Edwards, *Foundation for Management of Quality in the Western World*, p. 13.

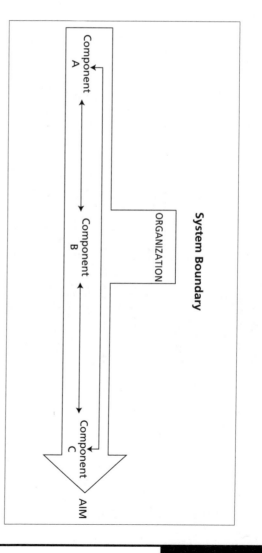

System Boundary

ORGANIZATION

Component A → Component B → Component C → AIM

This concept is new to me. When we optimize our own departments, we may be suboptimizing the entire company! Where does that leave competition between divisions? Someone has to lose. If someone loses, how can the corporation optimize its aim?

The Importance of Interdependence in a System

"The degree of interdependence between component processes may vary from one system to another. This concept was contributed by Dr. Barbara Lawton. A bowling team has low interdependence because it is composed of individual members whose scores are added.

"On the other hand, a fine orchestra is highly interdependent. The players are not there to play solos as prima donnas, to catch the ear of the listener. They are there to support each other. They are usually not the best players in the country. They work as a team under the leadership of the conductor."

An industrial engineer commented that an orchestra is very inefficient: some people are just sitting there counting. Only the conductor works all the way through. Less than 100 percent efficient. If the industrial engineer had his way, all the musicians would be playing all instruments all the time.

A business is more interdependent than an orchestra. Without teamwork, chaos is rampant. Lost orders, missing parts, and units that don't communicate eventually cause everything to grind to a halt.

"Management's job is to coordinate the activities of each component. It is their task to see to it that the activity of each component contributes to the aim of the system. Failure to achieve this coordination can optimize one or more components at the expense of the total system.

Component optimization often results in system suboptimization."

This is a novel idea. For years the focus was on individual contributions. How can I make my department the best? When my department does well, it might mean that another department might look bad, but who cares? The bonus of each department manager is based upon his unit's performance. Now, Dr. Deming is saying that anything less than a system-wide approach is a loser. This kind of thinking will shake things up at my company!

Degree of Interdependence

Bowling Team → Low Interdependence

Orchestra → Business → High Interdependence

An Example of the Systems Concept—Customer/Supplier Flowchart

"In the summer of 1950, Japanese management learned this flowchart. It was up in front of the room.

"They learned to see manufacturing as a process.

"They had great knowledge of statistics, chemistry, mathematics, among others, but no way to put it together.

"They learned how to use customer research."

On one page we are able to see all elements of a system. A complete corporation, division, company, department, branch, section, or work unit is shown as a system. How simple. This type of system-wide thinking, big-picture thinking, is so often missed. Yet it is critical to top management's job.

Manufacturing and Marketing as a System

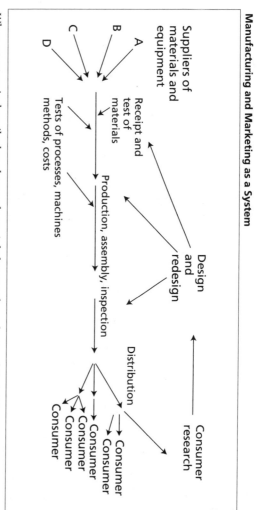

When a system is described as shown above, it helps people understand their jobs.

How to Suboptimize a Firm

Taking the Company Down the Tubes

Here is how Western management hurts itself:

- Everyone is kept in an adversarial position
- Each person, unit, department is ranked against each other
- Plants are pitted against one another
- Each supplier is the enemy
- Each work unit does its best and cares little of its impact on others
- When something goes wrong, work units strive to protect themselves from blame
- Each component passes products, information, and services over the wall. "Let the next guy figure it out. I've done my job. I met my specifications."

Manufacturing and Marketing as Adversary Subsystems

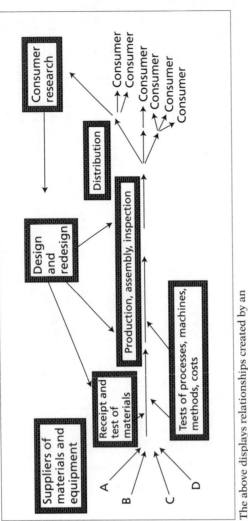

The above displays relationships created by an organizational chart rather than by seeing the company as a system. Organizational charts create walls around functions.

Theory of Variation

Profound Knowledge of the interaction of subsystems leads naturally to questions about their performance. To accomplish this, managers need some knowledge of variation, such as:

- Appreciation of a stable system.
- Understanding of special causes and common causes of variation.
- Knowledge that variation will always be there, between people, in output, in service, in product.
- Knowledge of the difference between a stable system and a capable system.
- Knowledge about the different kinds of uncertainty in statistical data.
- Two mistakes are possible in an attempt to improve a process:

  Mistake 1: Treat a common cause as though it were a special cause.

  Mistake 2: Treat a special cause as though it were a common cause.

- Knowledge of procedures aimed at minimum economic loss from these two mistakes (Shewhart Chart).

Data from a system can be analyzed and plotted. In addition to the data points, a plot of the upper and lower control limits (UCL and LCL) can be computed. A sample of a control chart appears in the illustration above.

When the process is stable or in control, all the data points will fall within the two limits. Those points are considered to come from a process that has only common causes of variation.

However, if one or more of the data points fall outside the control limits (or show certain patterns), those data points are said to come from a special or assignable cause of variation acting on the process.

It is the manager's job to know the difference. Without this basic knowledge, any management action will be mere tampering. Managers working hard, yet making things worse.

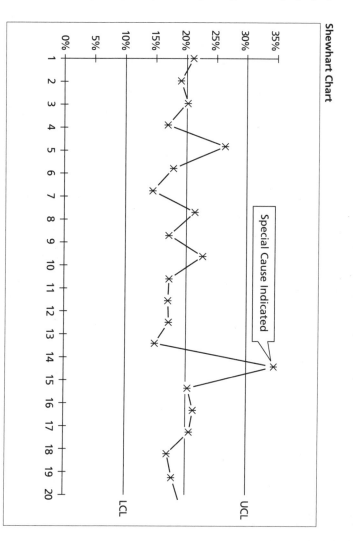

Shewhart Chart

Variation Is So Easy to Understand

"Patrick Nolan, then age 10, timed the arrival of the school bus."

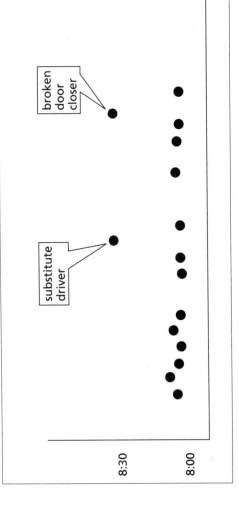

"What do you think happened when Patrick took this to school for the science fair? The teacher thought it was nonsense. Patrick's father, a well-known statistician, had to go to school to explain.

"The study of variation is exacting. There can be many such projects. How much variation is there in the scales in the grocery? Is a pound really a pound? Dial "time" in various cities and see how it agrees. TV stations agree to 1/100 of a second, they have to."

Theory of Knowledge

How many examples does it take to develop a theory?

☐ none
☐ one
☐ ten
☐ —————— (fill in)

None. A thousand examples won't make a theory, yet a single unexplained failure will overthrow a theory. When an example overthrows a theory, we don't have to discard the theory entirely, we may revise it.

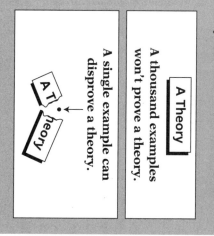

| A Theory |

A thousand examples won't prove a theory.

A single example can disprove a theory.

Management, to be successful, must be able to predict, with some confidence, the future. To do this we need a theory about specific future behavior. For instance:

"Gravity is a pretty good theory. It seems to work every time. It is cheap. (Laughter) But just one contradictory example could overthrow that theory."

We have a theory of gravity, we predict that it will work and we can use this theory to build other theories.

Another example is the answer to the question, "How will I drive home this evening?" One can predict that one's automobile will start up and run satisfactorily and plan accordingly.

Theory leads to questions. Without the right questions, experience and examples teach nothing.

We shoot from the hip at times; without the benefit of Profound Knowledge, twenty years of experience may only be one year of experience twenty times over (or less).

DAY ONE

There Is No Such Thing As a True Value

The Cost of Goods Sold =
Beginning Inventory +
Purchases – Closing Inventory.

In the illustration, the Beginning Inventory is $40,000 for 250,000 units. Each month the price increased. The company purchased 500,000 units per month. At the end of the time, the value of goods available for sale was $590,000. During this time period, 2,000,000 units were sold. What is the Cost of Goods Sold?

It depends on how we value the Closing Inventory. Two common methods, First In, First Out (FIFO) and Last In, First Out (LIFO) are illustrated in the diagram. The FIFO method results in a residual inventory of $190,000. The LIFO method yields $130,000. There is no such thing as a true value. There exists only the result of a procedure.

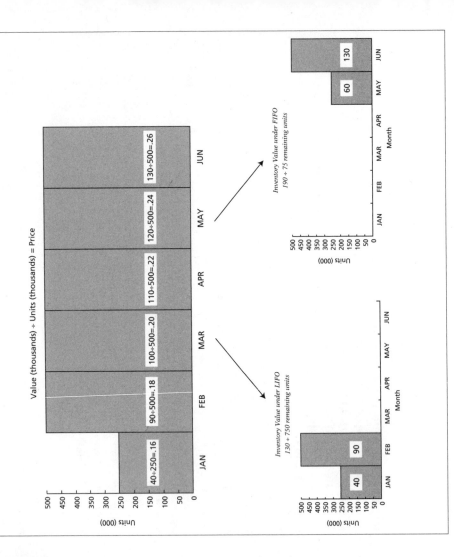

Value (thousands) ÷ Units (thousands) = Price

JAN 40÷250=.16 FEB 90÷500=.18 MAR 100÷500=.20 APR 110÷500=.22 MAY 120÷500=.24 JUN 130÷500=.26

Inventory Value under LIFO
130 + 750 remaining units

Inventory Value under FIFO
190 + 75 remaining units

Psychology

Intrinsic motivation: This is the motivation that comes from within people. We have choked it off.

Extrinsic motivation: This is external motivation from outside factors. Our system of rewards has ruined us. We have tried extrinsic motivation on a huge scale in Northern America. Our emphasis on extrinsic motivation has smothered intrinsic motivation. **Over-justification** can destroy intrinsic motivation.

"Dr. Joyce Orsini tells the story about a little boy who took it into his head to wash dishes each night. His mom decided to put him on the payroll, so she paid him a quarter each night. He never washed another dish. (Laughter)

"He was proud. He had intrinsic motivation, and the payment destroyed his motivation."

When washing dishes, the boy contributed to the family. No amount of money could pay for this. When the mother set a value on the work, she killed the intrinsic motivation. It was a case of over-justification.

"In our so-called merit systems everyone has his own life preserver. It's each man for himself.

"Everyday I hear of companies that are dropping the merit system."

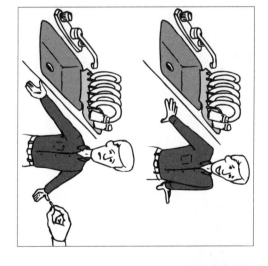

It must be kept in mind that reward systems have to be carefully selected to avoid the problem of over-justification. A specific review of the problems associated with bonus and gain-sharing is treated by Dr. Joyce Orsini in her article, "Bonuses: What is the Impact?" *National Productivity Review,* Spring 1987.

DAY ONE

Reflections During Lunch

This is the first half day of a four-day seminar and Dr. Deming has already raised serious questions in my mind regarding what we have done over the past three years. I really didn't think that improving quality would be such a far-reaching proposition.

At my company we have an elaborate system of management by objectives. We do much "negotiating of goals," then we all figure how to be sure we look good on paper when review time comes. Right before the review, people will do anything to ensure that their individual or group goals are met on paper. To heck with anyone else.

As we get close to the end of the quarter I've seen items shipped that were not ready. We just needed to make our numbers, so we let the field people do the finishing at the customer's location. Who can calculate the loss?

I know one plant manager who refused to make a run change for a customer because he knew that it would hurt his monthly efficiencies. To make the run change he would have had to take his production line down for five hours. It was better for his MBO to force the customer to go to our competitor for the parts. I can't blame him. Top management focuses on the MBO, the bottom line, the efficiency scores.

Then someone sold top management on the idea of customer satisfaction ratings linked with our performance reviews. Customers received questionnaires asking for rating of the sales force. Each year when those ratings went out the sales force would give away the store to get a good rating. Top management was only doing its best, thinking they were increasing customer satisfaction, no one would dare tell them how the overall system worked.

One year, top management was really worried about the quarterly dividend. They knew that if the stock went down the Board would be mad. They found some consultants who offered quick action. The easiest way to improve the profit was to cut costs. (It's as if no one thought the best way was to increase sales!!) At the plant level the consultants walked around and asked what everyone does. Then they made some simplistic measurements, having no clue about the concept of variation. These consultants then recommended the elimination of jobs. What havoc it caused. We are still trying to recover. It will be years before we figure out what happened.

3

Obligations 1 through 5

Obligation 1—Constancy of Purpose

How can Western management transform itself? We need a theory of management. Dr. Deming now presents a management theory for the improvement of quality, productivity, and competitive position. This theory of management consists of 14 obligations. These are obligations of all levels of management, from the top down.

Why do workers and managers need to know the organization's mission? So they can plan for the future.

Management must state its long-term purpose; it can change, but not with the wind! (Not change each day, not latch onto the next fad, not jump ship every time sales decline.)

Everyone needs to know his long-term intentions:

 Employees need to know
 Suppliers need to know
 Customers need to know

Management should publish a policy that says, "No one will lose their job due to better quality."

A mission statement should state some social value. It is not enough to say we are in business to make umbrellas. The business is to provide protection from the elements.

A good question to ask is, "Where do you want your business to be five or ten years from now?"

The temptation is to give an easy answer. To avoid this trap, Mr. W. A. Golomski suggests that you answer the following question:

"Give the details of how you will accomplish this transformation."

Below is the mission statement of a trucking firm, G.O.D. (Guaranteed Overnight Delivery).

Mission Our mission is to consistently prosper by benefiting our customers through continuous improvement of our unique transportation service.

Values The company will provide an environment for its people that promotes joy in work, achievement of personal goals, and an opportunity to share in our prosperity.

 We are a team and treat each other with trust and respect.

 The conduct of our company must be pursued in a manner that is socially responsible and commands respect for its integrity and positive contributions to society.

Obligation 2—Adopt the New Philosophy

The new philosophy is that we can no longer live with the levels of quality that we were able to tolerate in the past. Consumers are becoming more demanding and the firm of tomorrow must meet these demands.

The effect of quality on productivity is shown in the first line of the chain reaction diagram. Another way of looking at this is to consider the economist's definition of productivity.

The economist's definition of productivity is

PRODUCTIVITY = $\frac{\text{OUTPUT}}{\text{INPUT}}$

If quality is poor then the output will be less to the extent that bad-quality items exist. The bad-quality items are still around and must either be scrapped or reworked. The cost of this activity is in the input.

When output is low and input is high, productivity is very low.

$$\downarrow P = \frac{O \downarrow}{I \uparrow}$$

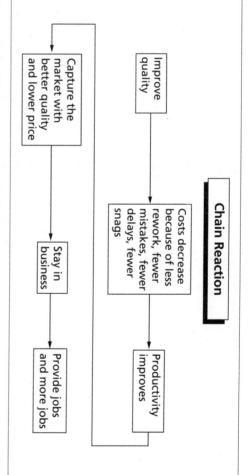

Chain Reaction

Improve quality → Costs decrease because of less rework, fewer mistakes, fewer delays, fewer snags → Productivity improves

Capture the market with better quality and lower price → Stay in business → Provide jobs and more jobs

Improve quality and you reverse this situation. Output goes up, input goes down, and productivity shoots up.

$$\Rightarrow P = \frac{O \uparrow}{I \downarrow}$$

Improving quality is a cheaper way to increase productivity than alternative methods such as automation. With automation, output goes up but so does input to pay for the automation. If productivity goes up at all, it increases slowly.

$$\uparrow P = \frac{O \uparrow}{I \uparrow}$$

Obligation 3—Cease Dependence on Mass Inspection

> We still need inspection, but we should not depend upon it.
>
> Some products must have inspection.
>
> Inspection is vital, but misused causes heavy loss.

"Sure, there will always be inspection, but let's do it right.

"One Monday morning, after hearing my lectures, a manager at Ford went back and fired all his inspectors. He spent the rest of the week trying to get them back!!" (Laughter)

Dr. Deming is often misunderstood on this point. The key word is "dependence." Dr. Harold Dodge said long ago that you cannot inspect quality into a product. Quality must be built into the product. If you depend on inspection to achieve quality, you fail to look at the process to improve it.

"I was told this story by a friend. He bought a coat. He found a total of 16 tags such as these:

Pockets Inspected
by No. 6

"But a pocket was not sewn! (Laughter) "Maybe the public loves inspection, but it won't fool us. We know better!! (Laughter)

"Give people a chance to understand the system. Then we won't need so much inspection."

The Hazard of 100 Percent Inspection

Most mistakes and defects are never found. To illustrate this effect, try counting the letter "F" or "f" in the top box. The answer is found on a page 52.

Federal Funds are the re-sult of years of years of scientific study combined with the experience of years

THREE MILE ISLAND

Ninety-eight percent of accidents are built into the system. Even at Three Mile Island, the engineers had filed reports in advance about the problems.

DAY ONE

When to Use Mass Inspection

Cost Method

There are times when you must use inspection. For instance, use 100 percent inspection when the process is stable yet the quality is not good enough. The decision is an economic one.

COST OF NOT INSPECTING

Number of items (n)	=		10,000
Times average percentage defective items ($\bar{p}$ [reads "p bar"])	= ×		.01
Total expected defective items ($n\bar{p}$)	=		100
Times cost of a nonconforming item (k_2)	= ×		$ 100
Total cost of nonconforming items			$10,000

COST OF INSPECTING

Number of items (n)	=		10,000
Times inspection cost per item (k_1[reads "k sub one"])	= ×		$ 5
Total cost to inspect			$50,000

Since inspection costs $50,000 to save the downstream cost of $10,000, it pays us not to inspect.

The General Formula

We can determine whether to inspect by examining the cost of inspecting one item (k_1) and comparing this cost to the downstream loss incurred (k_2) when a defect shows up later in assembly or gets into the hands of a customer.

The ratio of $k_1/k_2 = p^*$ [reads "p star"] is determined. The decision to inspect or not to inspect is based on a comparison of the cut-off criteria p^* to the process average, $\bar{p}$. The process average can be determined from a control chart of the process.

if p^* is less than $\bar{p}$ then do 100 percent inspection

if p^* is greater than $\bar{p}$ do not inspect.

Using the data in the example on the left, where

$k_1 = \$\ 5$
$k_2 = \$\ 100$
$\bar{p} = .01$ (or 1 percent)

the ratio

$$p^* = \frac{k_1}{k_2} = \frac{\$5}{\$100} = .05 \text{ (or 5 percent)};$$

p^* is greater than $\bar{p}$ =
.05 is greater than .01
therefore
DO NOT INSPECT.
This is the identical result achieved with the cost method of analysis.

Three Worlds—Rules for Inspection

	World One	World Two	World Three
	Cost is Infinite $k_2 = \infty$	Cost is between Infinity and 0 $\infty > k_2 > 0$	Cost is 0 $k_2 = 0$
Example	The work cannot be made perfectly. For instance: Tubes for nuclear reactors	The work cannot be made perfectly, for instance: Funds Transfer between banks	The work is done by a stable process with no defects.
Rule	No defects or mistakes may go out	Sewing seams in a garment There is a cost of inspection, k_1 and an additional cost, k_2 further down the line due to a bad item slipping past the inspector.	There is a cost of inspection, k_1.
Solution	100% inspection	If the process is stable with mean p, then see general inspection formula on previous page. If process is not stable, use the Joyce Orsini rules.* * see *Out of the Crisis*, p. 415	We need some inspection to construct the process control chart and make improvement possible.

k_2 = cost of an error escaping inspection

DAY ONE

Inspect the Process—Not the Product

Inspection of Product

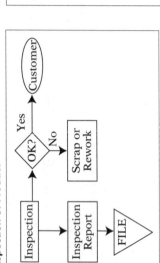

Inspection of the product to cull out defective items is both costly and not 100 percent effective. The illustration above shows the process of inspection to cull out defects.

The illustration on the right shows a preferred alternative. Use the data from the inspection to get information on the process. Then use the process data to improve on a continuous basis.

There are six Fs in the example from page 49. Is that what you found? Reading through the figure once is 100 percent inspection. Reading through the figure twice is 200 percent inspection. Most people find four or five Fs in one reading.

Inspection of Process

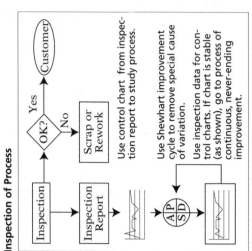

Use control chart from inspection report to study process.

Use Shewhart improvement cycle to remove special cause of variation.

Use inspection data for control charts. If chart is stable (as shown), go to process of continuous, never-ending improvement.

Federal Funds are the result of years of scientific study combined with the experience of years

Obligation 4—End the Practice of Awarding Business on the Basis of Price Tag Alone—Instead Reduce Cost by Reducing Variation

"It is a common practice to award business to the lowest bidder."

"We can't afford the losses from this practice."

"In the past, purchasing departments concentrated on cost of purchase and ignored cost of use."

"Is the purchasing manager's job to look at price tags only?"

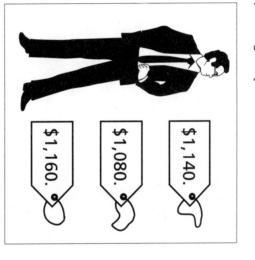

Some purchasing agents look at price tags but are blind to total cost.

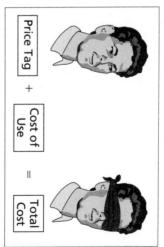

| Price Tag | + | Cost of Use | = | Total Cost |

"To give business to lowest bidder is a dubious practice. It assumes that all quality characteristics can be described in the specification. It doesn't work in our world.

"If every one of 17 suppliers gave you exactly the same product, then you'd be a fool not to buy from the lowest bidder."

Buying on Price Tag Alone

The purchasing department has the job of cooperating with the rest of the company.

"A woman called me from Chicago. She wished to meet me at 9 or 10 A.M. in New York City. She would arrive at 7:00 A.M. Her flight was two hours. Furthermore, there was a change in time zones.

"I asked her why she would arrive so early; couldn't she get another flight? 'No,' she said, 'her travel department made the arrangements.' The company saves $138, by making her awake at 2 in the morning!

"But what about the loss? Does anyone care? How can a person, who must awake at 2:00 A.M., work? This is an example of suboptimization." (*Audience murmurs in agreement as people tell each other horror stories about purchasing departments.*)

"Isn't it management's job to know the effect of their policies?"

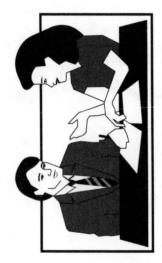

"It is more trouble to find out the needs, it is more difficult; it requires digging.

"Who would buy an automobile tire based solely on the price tag? What people want is trouble-free miles per dollar."

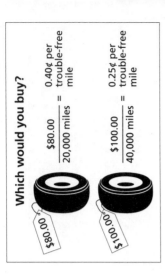

Which would you buy?

$$\frac{\$80.00}{20{,}000 \text{ miles}} = 0.40¢ \text{ per trouble-free mile}$$

$$\frac{\$100.00}{40{,}000 \text{ miles}} = 0.25¢ \text{ per trouble-free mile}$$

"How could we know that each tire would give trouble-free miles? That is the job of the purchasing agent: to dig and find the answers."

Comparison of Suppliers

What is the aim of the purchasing department?

- lowest initial cost, or
- lowest lifetime cost

The lowest lifetime cost can be achieved by striving toward uniformity.

At a chemical company that makes parts for the auto industry, when asked about the purchasing of incoming material management said:

"We can learn to use almost anything that you send us, if you only keep it relatively uniform, batch after batch, day after day, week after week. Of course, the closer it is to the nominal or desired value, the better it is for us. "If you keep changing the product, we can't learn how to use it . . ."

Purchasing must learn that it is not a question of buying on price tag alone. The total cost, the cost of the price tag, and the cost of using the item (affected by quality) must be considered. Buy that which gives the lowest total life-cycle cost.

"Did you ever ask workers, what is the loss when you change suppliers?

"Some will tell you one hour, three hours, three days, three weeks. The loss varies.

"Does anybody care? Why are we willing to live with these losses?"

The desired or nominal value of the product is 350 with a plus or minus 250 specification. Supplier A provides product with mean of 250 and standard deviation of 50. Supplier B supplies product with mean of 350 and standard deviation of 83.3. The price tag is the same for both suppliers. From which supplier, A or B, would you buy? You need to draw a loss function to know. (See next page)

"Management's job is to know."

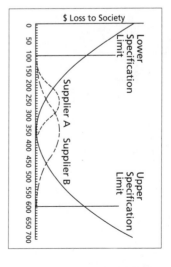

The authors are grateful to Dr. Madhav S. Phadke for his review of this and the following page and for his helpful suggestions.

Readers interested in learning more about the loss function and its use are referred to Dr. Phadke's book, *Quality Engineering Using Robust Design* (Prentice Hall, 1989). Some other texts covering the loss function are Taguchi, Genichi, *Introduction to Quality Engineering* (Asia Productivity Organization, 1986) and Creveling, C. M. and William Fowlkes, *Engineering Methods for Robust Design: Advanced Taguchi Methods* (Addison-Wesley 1995).

Taguchi's Use of the Loss Function

Buy A or B?

Buy Lowest Total Cost = Price Tag plus Average Quality Loss. Buy B since the Price Tag is the same and the Average Quality Loss for B is $6,889 \times C$, which is less than for A = $12,500 \times C$.

Q = Average Quality Loss

$Q = \{s^2 + [M - t]^2\}C$, where

Q = Loss Function

C = Constant

s^2 = variance of curve

M = Mean of curve

t = Nominal (target)

The Specifications are

Nominal (t) = 350 units

Specification Limit:

Lower (LSL) = 100 units

Upper (USL) = 600 units

For Curve A, the mean and standard deviation, (s), are

M = 250 units

s = 50 units

$Q_A = \{s^2 + [M - t]^2\}C$

$Q_A = \{50^2 + [250 - 350]^2\}C$

$Q_A = \{2,500 + 10,000\}C$

$Q_A = 12,500 \times C$

For Curve B, the mean and standard deviation, (s), are

M = 350 units

s = 83 units

$Q_B = \{83^2 + [350 - 350]^2\}C$

$Q_B = \{6,889 + 0\}C$

$Q_B = 6,889 \times C$.

I was afraid I'd have to do some math. But, actually if I take my time and use my calculator I can follow along.

Obligations 1 through 5

Three Worlds for Purchasing

	World One	World Two	World Three
Customer	Customer knows his wants and communicates them.	Customer knows his wants and communicates them.	Customer thinks he knows his wants and can communicate them. However, he is willing to consider advice and make possible changes.
Supplier	Several suppliers can supply these needs exactly. All can do equal production and service at different prices. Price paid is the only cost.	Several suppliers can supply these needs exactly at the same price, but one gives better service.	Several qualified suppliers quote prices, all different. Price paid is not the only cost. The cost of use is a factor. Supplier must have knowledge, training, capacity, bank credit.
Decision	Anyone would be a fool not to buy at the lowest price.	Customer gives order to the one with better service.	The customer cannot work with more than one. The customer may think of long-term improvements. He must enter into a long-term arrangement. He may consider a single supplier. On what basis? How important is the customer to the supplier? What knowledge does the supplier have about product and its use? If unable to decide, do business with two or three suppliers until you can come to a decision on a single supplier.

Reduce Variation through Long-Term Relationships

In long-term relationships both supplier and customer have a chance to learn from each other.

Old Way

- One year contracts
- Lowest bidder
- Adversary

New Way

- **Long-term contracts or commitments**
- **Lower and lower costs**
- **Continual improvement of quality**
- **Both can learn from each other**
- **Partnership**
- **Continual adjustment and improvement**

"Why even try to improve? A supplier would be a fool to try to improve if someone else will get the order anyway."

How do you choose a supplier for a long-term relationship?

"He must have a burning desire to work with you. He must also have knowledge about your business. Be careful in selection. Trust can't be acquired without risk.

"You cannot work with two suppliers. (You can't even work with one!) (Laughter)

"Don't leave your suppliers alone. Continuously interact with your suppliers. They don't have the same degree of knowledge. Some have more knowledge than the customer."

Things to consider when working with a supplier:

- ☐ Do they have quality?
- ☐ Do they have capacity?
- ☐ Can they expand?
- ☐ Can they handle expansion?
- ☐ Will you support them during expansion?
- ☐ Will bankers give them money?

There is no sure way.

What About the Purchase of a Commodity

Dr. Deming is now discussing a topic that is controversial and goes against many existing practices. The entire idea of single source supply is new. The audience asks: What about purchasing a commodity?

> Buying sugar in little packets is different then buying it by the ton.

> What if I want to buy sugar?

> Do I want it in little packets or in bulk?

"Little packets are 998/1,000 part sucrose. The other parts are other types of sugars. Prices are posted on the Chicago and the London exchange. You can always beat the market if you wait, shop around, be patient. So how would you buy it? What would you want to know?"

- Do the suppliers have it in stock?
- When would it be delivered?

  This Thursday?
  Next Thursday?

- Will it come in a clean truck?
- Will the driver help me unload?
- Will the invoice be accurate?
- Will my payment be readily credited and properly posted by his accounting department?

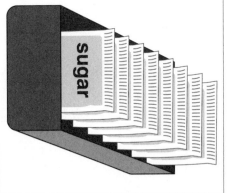

"Beware of conference room promises."
(Ronald Moen)

59

Single Supplier Policy

WRONG! A single supplier with two plants supplying one plant of a customer increases the variability.

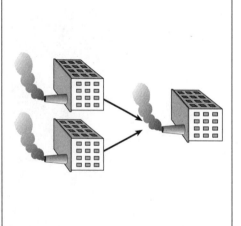

Good! One supplier's plant serves one customer's plant.

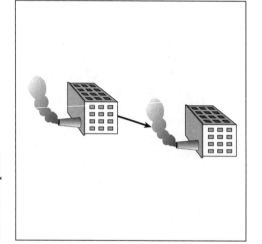

Good! Each supplier plant serves a specific plant of the customer.

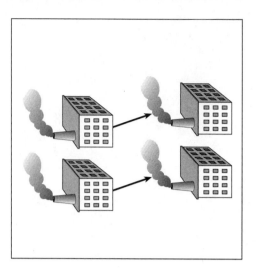

What If Your Supplier Has a Fire

The audience seems nervous about the idea of a single supplier. They think that maybe Dr. Deming has gone too far. Surely what they learned in business school about the benefits of multi-source supplies must be valid. How will Dr. Deming explain this?

"General Motors once had a fire in a transmission plant. What happened? They had a genuine crisis. They sent a crew to the plant and removed the dies. The dies were taken to a competitor's plant, which then went to three shifts. They worked around the clock to make up for the lost plant. Truckers would drive all night to deliver the parts. Production did not stop. Sure it was difficult.

"GM's competitors helped. We do have a social memory from a friendly competitor that doesn't try to choke us."

"If you think one supplier is bad, two suppliers give you twice as many problems. Make an arrangement with your single supplier so that if he has a problem, he will help you find another supplier.

"I received a letter that read: 'We had a fire in Dayton, Ohio. Fifty-one competitors offered help. We moved in with one. Found room for forty men. People came to help us out . . .' People came to the rescue of a worthy competitor.

"By the way, where do you have the most fires?

"In fire-proof buildings!" (Laughter)

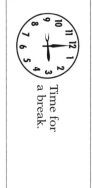

Time for a break.

Obligation 5—Continual Improvement

Dr. Deming asks: "Where have big improvements been made?"

Audience: Aircraft   Medicine   Agriculture

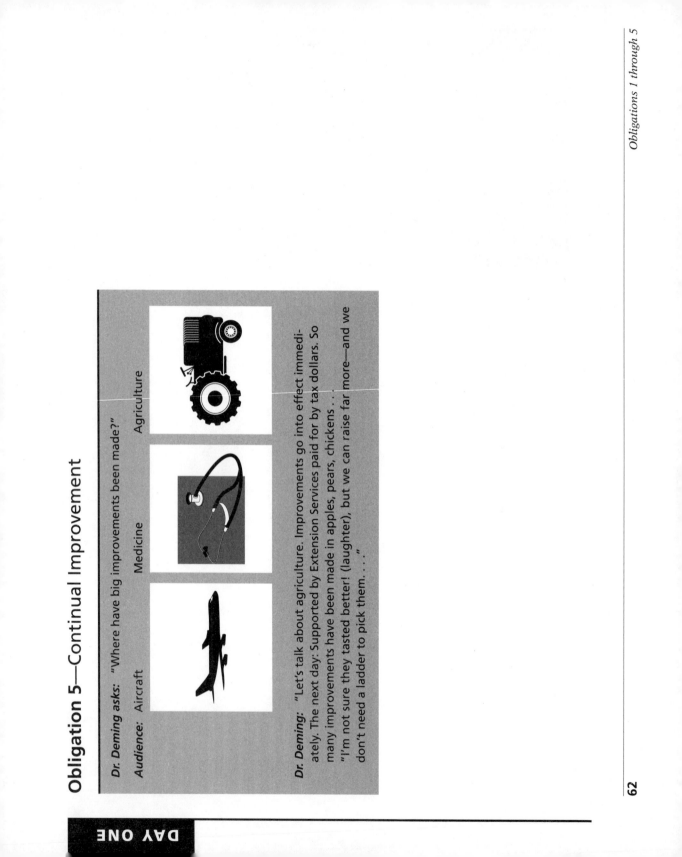

Dr. Deming: "Let's talk about agriculture. Improvements go into effect immediately. The next day. Supported by Extension Services paid for by tax dollars. So many improvements have been made in apples, pears, chickens . . .

"I'm not sure they tasted better! (laughter), but we can raise far more—and we don't need a ladder to pick them. . . ."

Innovation and Improvement

Management's job is to create a climate in which everyone can take joy in his workplace by:

1. Innovation of product and service
2. Innovation of process
3. Improvement of existing products and services
4. Improvement of existing processes.

"An example of the wrong way involves an executive who writes:

'Our people in the plants are responsible for their own product quality.'

"WRONG! People on the production floor can do little to improve quality. Once it gets to the production floor it is too late to do much about quality.

"A machine needs oil but the operator can't buy it; he uses the oil issued to him.

"Another company with the wrong approach writes:

'Quality is the responsibility of the operator. The inspector shares that responsibility. The inspector will use Military Specification 105D.'

"This is WRONG. It encourages us to accept a certain number of defects per thousand. Just salt them in." (Laughter)

Where Does Innovation Come From

"Did customers ask for electric light? NO.

"They never asked for it. The producer produced it.

"Did a customer ask for pneumatic tires? The first ones were not very good, I remember them well. (Laughter)

"No one asked for a car, nor a telephone. No one asked for a copying machine or a fax machine.

"Innovation does not come from the customer. Innovation comes from the producer, from people who are responsible for themselves and have only themselves to satisfy."

Dr. Deming says: "Once in my youth (when I was only 75) (Laughter) I thought that innovation came from monopolies or fortresses of power. But then I began to think that economic independence fosters innovation. Self-esteem is what grows innovation.

"Self-esteem is destroyed by the merit system and MBO by which one person in a company learns that he can get ahead by pushing the other guy down.

"When one company was shown the xerox process, they called in a marketing consultant who said, 'This is an interesting idea, but it won't sell, we have carbon paper.'" (Laughter)

Dr. Deming is helping us to look beyond our typical approaches, to look at the subject of innovation and constant improvement.

"Faraday's diary (1810–1820) indicated he was responsible for himself. Did anyone ask for magnetism?"

Obligations 1 through 5

The Shewhart Cycle for Learning and Improvement

On page 5 we described the Shewhart cycle. This cycle is a driving force for innovation. There are two aspects to this cycle. In one format, the cycle is a consumer cycle. This is the cycle that helps us to understand what to do for improvement. The other aspect is the cycle of learning (PDSA). This is where the cycle helps us achieve improvement. The two are related and are both important.

The consumer cycle is used in planning innovation and improvement. An example of the use of this cycle is the Toyota experience. When Toyota first entered the American car market it was with the Toyopet. This vehicle was underpowered, the headlights were not bright enough, the interiors were stark, the ride was harsh, and it didn't sell. They pulled it from the market, studied the success of the Volkswagen Beetle and then returned with the Corolla years later. By testing the product in service, Toyota learned what would improve the car to make the customer happier.

They then used the second facet of the Shewhart cycle to help the engineers to achieve product improvement (shown below).

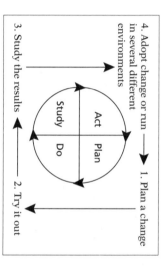

4. Adopt change or run ——▶ 1. Plan a change
in several different
environments

3. Study the results   2. Try it out

In the United States we rush through the cycle at great speed. The part of the cycle that is most important, "Plan," is given short shrift. Many managers test first and design later. In the process they suboptimize the cycle of learning. A statistician can be of great help in the planning, execution, and analysis of an experiment. The statistician will ask questions of the experts in the subject matter—questions such as, "What is the purpose of the test?" "How does it fit into the corporate statement of constancy of purpose?" "If these are the results [some hypothetical outcome], what actions will you take?" These and other questions are often neglected by management in their planning.

Once the test has been designed properly, try it out, preferably on a small basis. Have the statistician design a method of determining that the test was carried out as planned.

When the results are available, study them. Study the results, taking one of three actions: 1. Accept the change; 2. Reject the change; or 3. There are not enough data from the test to come to a conclusion, therefore, redesign the test and repeat it.

"Do the experiments under different conditions. We want to be able to predict but we can't be sure. If I let go of this pen, I have a high degree of belief that it will fall. It has always been the case!" (Laughter)

Evening Study Group

At 4:00 P.M. Dr. Deming says, "I'm now going to turn over the session to Mr. Latzko. This is the most important part of your day. You will work hard . . . until midnight on the questions."

Mr. Latzko explains the procedure. Form groups of six people. They need not be from the same company. In fact, it may be good if they were not all from the same firm. Introduce yourselves to the other members of your group. See the Epilogue for a list of questions and how to use them. Every member of the group will read through all questions pertaining to Day One. As a group, select at least five questions for discussion. Following the discussion, choose two of the five questions for response tomorrow morning. Write, on the cards provided, summaries of the consensus or lack thereof of the group on these two questions. Use one card per question. Return the completed cards to the helpers.

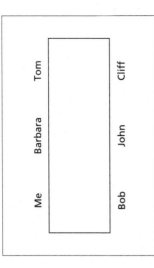

This is an interesting group I am with. Are they stubborn! I had a tough time getting everyone to focus on the question "Explain why everybody loses from failure to optimize the system."

We already had dinner and we are still talking. There is much food for thought.

What a day this has been. I came because I knew that I had to do something. Competition is all around us. The situation is bad. I had no idea that the general conditions were even worse than I thought. It was certainly revealing to hear about our import and export problems.

When Dr. Deming talked about the need to transform Western management I was very uneasy. Many of the problems he outlined were things that I have been doing all my life. I was taught to do things that way. However, when I think about it, it does seem to be wrong.

This system of Profound Knowledge really excited me. I thought I knew something about systems but Dr. Deming made many things clear to me. To think that I studied statistics and never used them. I couldn't wait to finish that

course. I memorized all the formulas to pass the test and forgot them as soon as I could. Now I find out this is important knowledge for managers. I better look at this topic again.

Reflections on Day One

That business about the theory of knowledge was interesting. There is no such thing as a true value. Well, if that is so, how can we see do business? I hope that Dr. Deming will talk more about that. Come to think about it, maybe that is the reason we have that big contract dispute. They measure one way, we measure differently.

I knew that we needed to know psychology. I'm a bit of a psychologist. Every salesman and manager is one. However, this concept of intrinsic motivation really struck a chord with me.

The business about mission statements is OK. We have a statement. I am going to review it in light of this session. It is much too long for everyone in the company to know it. Never mind using it. Dr. Deming is certainly right that we can no longer tolerate the levels of quality we used to get away with. That is why I am here.

That business about inspection was a shock. I always relied on the inspection to catch the bad work. I didn't realize how much that costs and how ineffective it is.

The concept of single supplier was fascinating. I couldn't help but think that we want to be the single supplier to our customers. We certainly can see the advantage from that viewpoint. However, when we choose suppliers we are inconsistent. I have to look into that when I get back.

Naturally we work to improve all the time. It just seems that we are always worrying about the outcomes instead of the process. I want the operations people to learn this.

I wonder how we teach our workers their job? This is another point I have to look into. So many great simple things to do and they all make sense. This seminar has been amazing so far.

- 100% versus no inspection
- lowest price versus lifetime cost
- profound knowledge versus no knowledge

4

Obligations 6 through 9

DAY FOUR | DAY THREE | DAY TWO | DAY ONE

Hands against the Wall

Day two begins at 8 A.M. Working groups make presentations. Dr. Deming's helpers selected them based on the work turned in the previous evening. They selected only a few of the hundreds of responses.

Dr. Deming takes part in these presentations. Sometimes he questions a presenter to emphasize a point. He often makes notes to himself.

On completion of the presentations, Dr. Deming rises and says, "Everybody up. Hands against the wall." He then leads the group in a few minutes of calisthenics.

"Turn counter-clockwise. Return.
"Turn clockwise. Return.
"Lower arms, inhale. Raise arms, exhale.
"Rotate arms.
"Tie your shoelaces, slowly. Careful, don't hurt yourself.
"Back up. Slowly.
"OK, everybody sit."

Obligation 6—Training for a Skill

People learn in different ways.

- Some learn from written words
- Others want to hear it
- Others learn by pictures
- Still others learn by demonstration

Once a person gets his performance in a stable state, further lessons will not help. He will have variation.

"It is no disgrace to learn one way or another. We must take into account the fact that people learn differently. This is management's job. Managers must also be teachers.

"I had a good friend, Harold Hotelling, who was a college professor. I would ask him questions but did not get answers. I discussed this with another friend, W. Allen Wallis. He suggested that I put my questions to Professor Hotelling in writing. It worked. Professor Hotelling could not understand the spoken word, but, when it was in writing, his response was brilliant.

"Many years ago another friend kept a record of his golf scores. From this record he made a control chart. He computed the average of every four consecutive games. For each set of four games, he computed the range. From these data, he computed a control chart. (See the next page for a chart of averages.) The top left chart shows several points falling outside the control limits. This indicates an unstable system.

"My friend took lessons. After the lessons he again computed the result of every four games and created a new control chart. This chart shows improvement. (See the top chart, right panel.)

"The result was an improved average (lower average score). There was less variability as shown by the narrower limits. His game was more consistent.

"In this next situation (see bottom chart), you can see that the golfer was already stable and new lessons were of no help."

Why a Leader Must Be a Trainer

The leader's job is to know who needs training and who does not. How can a leader know?

Anyone who has brought work to a state of statistical control, whether well trained or badly trained, is in a pattern. He has learned all that can be learned of that particular job. It is not economical to try to provide further training of the same kind. He may, nevertheless, with good training, learn very well some other kind of job.

"Have you ever met a golf player who was happy?

"I once played a game myself in 1929. I lost the ball and quit." (Laughter)

Consider again the chart drawn by the golfer. Each point on the chart is the average of four successive games. The center line is the average of all averages. The UCL and LCL are calculated from the data.

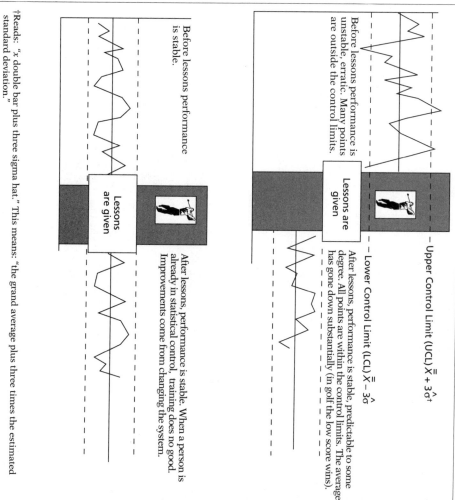

Before lessons performance is unstable, erratic. Many points are outside the control limits.

Lessons are given

After lessons, performance is stable, predictable to some degree. All points are within the control limits. The average has gone down substantially (in golf the low score wins).

— — Upper Control Limit (UCL) $\bar{\bar{X}} + 3\hat{\sigma}^\dagger$

— — Lower Control Limit (LCL) $\bar{\bar{X}} - 3\hat{\sigma}$

Before lessons performance is stable.

Lessons are given

After lessons, performance is stable. When a person is already in statistical control, training does no good. Improvements come from changing the system.

†Reads: "x double bar plus three sigma hat." This means: "the grand average plus three times the estimated standard deviation."

Obligation 7—Leadership

What is leadership?
What is the job of the manager?
What is the job of the supervisor?

"I had the privilege of working with my good friend and colleague David S. Chambers, now deceased, to help a plant superintendent to become a leader. The superintendent was just doing his best. He knew there was a problem with one of his production lines. He blamed his twenty-four people on that line. They made a lot of mistakes. If these people did not make mistakes, there would be none.

"Professor Chambers, a master, visited the production line and found that inspectors placed tickets listing defects in a pile. When the pile got too large they threw the bottom half in the trash!! (Laughter)

"Professor Chambers asked, could we take the bottom half? The superintendent was glad to help. Professor Chambers used these data to construct a simple chart of proportion defective. (See the chart marked "Before" on this page.) From the chart it was clear that the system was stable. It may

Before Developing Operational Definitions

not have been acceptable in the eyes of managers. It may have been too costly, but it was stable.

"Professor Chambers showed the chart to management. Because the system was stable, any real improvement must come from action on the system. That is the responsibility of management.

"He suggested that the managers and supervisors work at developing operational definitions of what made work acceptable. The managers and supervisors, through trial and error, developed the operational definitions. They created examples of conforming items and of nonconforming items. They posted the examples for everyone to see."

After Developing Operational Definitions

After developing operational definitions and training the workers, the results of entire system became better.

Many in the audience are wondering . . . What does he mean by stable? Maybe I should know that term? Is that the same as in control?

Doing Your Best is Not Good Enough

"Bob Dvorchak of the *San Diego Times* wrote an article (21 February 1983) on a survey of 970 historians who rated past presidents. The survey concluded that over half of our past presidents are above average. Historically, just think about it, over half of our presidents were above average!! (Laughter)

"Brian Joiner pointed out a newspaper article whose headlines announced "Half still under median . . ." It went on to explain that Union officials were complaining that despite increases, more than half of the league's players earned less that the league-wide median of $75,000 per year!! (Laughter)

"A teacher, only doing her best, writes that after two tests, the child was below average. The child thought that she was a failure. She needed remedial training to catch up in the class. What sense does this make? The teacher did not know that fully half the children will be below average on any test. What is the crime?"

Suppose there were sixteen children in the class; one-half, or eight, would be above average on test 1. Again, on test 2 about one-half or eight children would be above average. These are not necessarily the same children. Some would change from above to below average and vice-versa. The diagram below shows these changes.

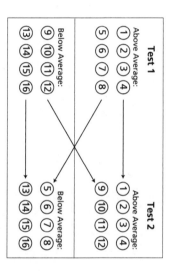

Test 1

Above Average:
① ② ③ ④
⑤ ⑥ ⑦ ⑧

Below Average:
⑨ ⑩ ⑪ ⑫
⑬ ⑭ ⑮ ⑯

Test 2

Above Average:
① ② ③ ④
⑨ ⑩ ⑪ ⑫

Below Average:
⑤ ⑥ ⑦ ⑧
⑬ ⑭ ⑮ ⑯

A teacher that does not understand variation would wrongly think that she had four genius type children (above average on both tests). She would erroneously think that four were improving (below average on test 1 and above average on test 2). She would erroneously judge four to be declining (above on test 1 and below on test 2). Lastly, she would erroneously think that four of the children were failures, below average on both tests.

"Could anything be worse?"

A leader:
1. Understands how the work of the group fits with the aims of the company.
2. Works with preceding stages and with following stages.
3. Tries to create joy in work for everybody.
4. Is a coach and counsel, not a judge.
5. Uses figures to help understand his people.
6. Works to improve the system that he and his people work in.
7. Creates trust.
8. Does not expect perfection.
9. Listens and learns.
10. Enables workers to do their job.

Obligation 8—Drive Out Fear

Dr. Deming begins this topic:

"I am thankful to Bill Latzko who, many years ago, pointed out to me the economic consequence of fear.

"You are entitled to a boss you can argue with, and respect. Captain [later General] Leslie Simon told me this. He would argue with his general for hours about a test procedure; but do it with respect. Argue with fact.

"How did I meet Captain Simon?! had the great fortune to work with Dr. Shewhart. An experience not to be duplicated. Often Dr. Shewhart would invite me to his home. That's where I met Captain Simon.

"I learned lot of what I know from Dr. Shewhart.

"Also, at the Bureau of the Census, we made great strides in accuracy. People came from throughout the world to learn."

When asked if he grades papers in his classes, Dr. Deming replied:

"I learn a lot from my students. I've taught since 1946. If a paper is due at the end of the term, and it is not ready, just send me a note. Some of the best papers come in a month late, two months late . . . I read the paper to learn about myself. How am I teaching? Grades are used for prediction, for selection. Who may proceed into the doctoral program . . . Who can tell?? I'm just catching up with some thoughts."

Dr. Deming suggests that arguing with a boss is OK, when done with respect. He is setting some new rules for the interaction of people.

Dr. Deming distinguishes between fear and anxiety. Fear occurs when the source is identifiable. Anxiety happens when the source is not identifiable.

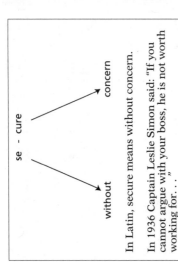

se - cure

without   concern

In Latin, secure means without concern.

In 1936 Captain Leslie Simon said: "If you cannot argue with your boss, he is not worth working for. . . ."

Blaming the Worker

The session organizers gave us a copy of Dr. Deming's book, Out of the Crisis, as well as a set of his notes. I frankly admit that I haven't opened the book until now. It is 507 pages, and I guess its been a long time since I read a book of this length.

On page 62 is a passage contributed by William W. Scherkenbach that describes exactly what happens in my company:

"A manager looks at a report of complaints by category. His eye falls on the highest figure on the paper, takes the telephone to wade in on the poor devil that is responsible for that category. This is another form of management by fear, and of management by numbers. Management's first step should be to discover by calculation, not by judgment, whether this category is out of control with respect to others. If yes, then this category requires his special attention and help. He must also work on the system to reduce all complaints."

In this lecture Dr. Deming reminded us that twenty years of experience is meaningless. It may be just one year of experience repeated twenty times!

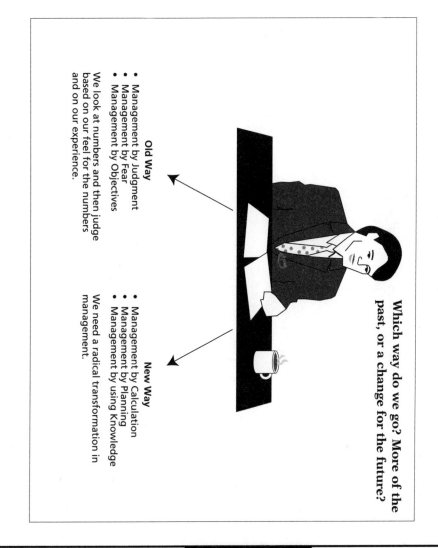

Which way do we go? More of the past, or a change for the future?

Old Way

- Management by Judgment
- Management by Fear
- Management by Objectives

We look at numbers and then judge based on our feel for the numbers and on our experience.

New Way

- Management by Calculation
- Management by Planning
- Management by using Knowledge

We need a radical transformation in management.

Obligation 9—Break Down Barriers between Staff Areas

Dr. Deming tells the story of three companies working for the same corporation all with separate presidents. This might be a good idea. It might also be a bad idea.

"Each makes parts for the other two. Each is measured by its own profit-and-loss sheet. They would pass product over the fence. Never mind the other fellow. Could they help each other? Yes, but each is too busy with its own problems."

This is the way it is in my company. We all work for the same corporation; we ship parts to each other. Yet the internal competition is greater than the external competition. We constantly blame each other for problems. If one of us makes improvements, it just creates problems for the others. We try to cooperate with each other, but we are usually just too busy with our day-to-day problems.

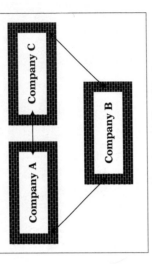

Company A, B, and C are all within the same corporation and they compete instead of cooperate.

DAY TWO

Why Don't People within an Organization Cooperate

Dr. Deming continues: "People in design don't talk to people in consumer research. Why not?

"It would look like they didn't know their job if they asked for help. Think about the loss to the company. Yet, the company is doing well. The company as a whole makes a profit, but that doesn't make it right."

At my company this is certainly a problem. One hand doesn't know what the other is doing. This results in many problems. What solution does Dr. Deming suggest?

Dr. Deming is suggesting that people work together. They need to be free of fear of taking a risk. We have teams in my company but they are almost always without the power to take a risk. They are second guessed. No wonder they get so little done.

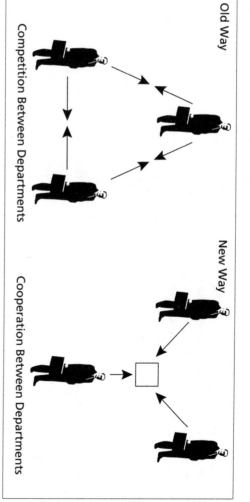

Old Way

Competition Between Departments

New Way

Cooperation Between Departments

I have heard of teams that function the way Dr. Deming describes. I heard that some companies are using a method called 'Simultaneous Engineering' or another technique that goes by the name of 'Quality

Function Deployment' (QFD). This method involves teams of the type described by Dr. Deming to solve problems of the future. I wonder if we could use these concepts. I will check when I get back.

Independent Kingdoms versus Cross-functional Teams

Dr. Deming suggests that we can accomplish a lot more through cooperation.

Over the years, corporate management has followed practices that create the walls of the independent kingdoms.

By playing one department against another, top management creates the walls that prevent cooperation.

Organization charts also play a role in creating the walls between departments. They define the kingdoms.

Management must learn that these practices are destructive to the organization.

Management can create an atmosphere of cooperation. The use of a flowchart as shown on page 37 makes clear everyone's job. In fact, the discussion of systems and optimization on pages 37–38 relates directly to what management must do to remove the barriers that exist today. Without the barriers, productivity improves—as many corporations have discovered.

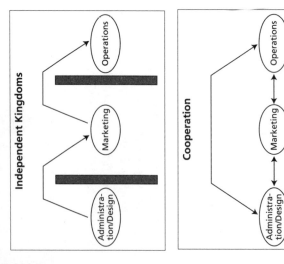

We Need a Theory of Cooperation

Dr. Deming asks:

"What time is it?"

Audience answers:

"Ten-fifteen . . ."

Dr. Deming adds:

"Ten-fifteen Greenwich Mean Time. Used by friend and foe alike. Cooperation worldwide."

Dr. Deming asks:

"What is the date?"

Audience answers:

"June 2nd."

Dr. Deming corrects:

"2nd June established by the International Date Line. Used the world over.

"Cooperation is what we have to learn.

"That is what we need to make progress."

Dr. Deming illustrates his point: "I have a flashlight—it takes two triple A batteries. I can buy them anywhere in the world. That's cooperation."

Other examples are the metric system and the European Community; i.e., a common weather station for all of Europe.

The focal point of a lens is set through voluntary standards. Then, off the cuff, Dr. Deming quickly gives us a lesson in optics. He draws the following diagram to illustrate his point.

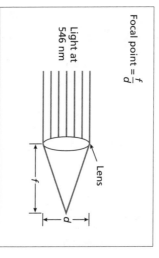

Focal point $= \dfrac{f}{d}$

Light at
546 nm

Lens

Cooperation Will Lead to More Standards

We need thousands of standards, so we can produce better products. With better products we will make more profit.

There is nothing wrong with profit earned.

People in business are entitled to a profit.

People in industry are treated as second class citizens—they should be treated as first class citizens.

Dr. Deming makes the point that businessmen in the United States are afraid to talk to each other. They are afraid of anti-trust laws, and this fear leads to a lack of cooperation.

"Why are we so worried about cooperation? With cooperation everyone wins. Prices are lower and markets are created.

"We are laboring under the misapprehension that competition solves problems. It does not, competition creates problems.

"Contribution from [Professor] William G. Ouchi.* He was the guest speaker at the annual meeting of a U. S. trade association. The place was Florida, the audience was 300 or so leaders of companies in the industry. The audience adjourned at noon for golf. Next noon the audience adjourned for fishing. Dr. Ouchi's speech the third day commenced as follows:

"While you are out on the golf course this afternoon, waiting for your partner to tee up, I want you to think about something. Last month I was in Tokyo, where I visited your trade association counterpart. It represents the roughly 200 Japanese companies who are your direct competitors. They are now holding meetings from eight each morning until nine each night, five days a week, for three months straight, so one company's oscilloscope will connect with another company's analyzer, so they can agree on product safety standards to recommend to the government (to speed up getting to the marketplace), so they can agree on their needs for changes in regulation, export policy, and financing and then approach their government with one voice to ask for cooperation. Tell me who you think is going to be

in better shape five years from now, you or your Japanese competitors?"

Note: Soon after the lecture a newspaper article revealed that Japanese companies had just reached agreement on the electronic architectural standards that would allow for the production of video still cameras for the American market. They expected to bring this new product to the commercial market by 1990.

*Taken from William G. Ouchi, *The M-Form Society* (Addison-Wesley, 1984), as quoted in W. Edwards Deming, *Out of the Crisis*, (Massachusetts Institute of Technology, Center for Advanced Engineering Study, 1986), p. 307.

Cooperation and Darwin

Thoughts during coffee break: We need a new theory. We need a theory of cooperation.

Most of us think Darwin's Theory supports competition, that survival of the fittest means that we all compete, on nature's business battlefield. A true study of Darwin's Theory shows that he talks about the outstanding degree of cooperation in the animal kingdom.

A recent study of skeletal remains of prehistoric saber-tooth tigers found many cats that sustained terrible hurt. Even though they had broken legs, dislocated hips, severe back damage and chronic arthritic conditions they survived. This suggests a theory of cooperation even

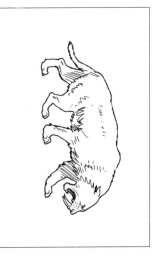

among fierce predators. It is plain that the others of the species allowed a disabled cat to limp after its fellows as they hunted and to feed on scraps. (As reported in the New York Times 26 September 1989.)

Coffee break at 10:15 A.M.

DAY TWO

5

The Red Beads

DAY FOUR | DAY THREE | DAY TWO | DAY ONE

The Workers Are Instructed

On return from morning break, Dr. Deming announces: "We are going into business. We have customers. We are going to set up a factory. We need willing workers. Also we need a secretary, two inspectors, and a chief inspector. I will be the foreman . . ."

Dr. Deming is full of surprises. We started the day by pulling apart the idea of buying on lowest bid, (something my company has been doing for years). Now we are going to do a simulation.

I'm the CEO of my company. I don't do hands-on work any more. There is no one here from the company to see me if I fail. It might be fun to show them how to play this game. OK, I'll volunteer . . .

Dr. Deming describes the system:

"You will be trained. Procedures are rigid, we know our business. We want no variation. Raw materials come in each day. They are a mixture of red and white beads. They arrive in a large vessel.

"Your job is to pour the beads from the large vessel to a smaller vessel. Let gravity do the work!! Gravity is cheap. And, it works every time. (Laughter) We have work standards, 50 beads per day. No more, no less.

"Our inspectors are independent. (The only thing we do right!!) Each inspector will examine production and look for defective beads, if any. The chief inspector will compare the answers of each inspector and in a loud voice will call out the number of defective beads.

"The secretary will record the results. We believe in measurement."

The Red Beads—Production—Day 1

It is a strange situation, being in front of five hundred people playing a game. Well, everyone appears to be having fun.

Dr. Deming asks our names and has the secretary write them on a data sheet.

Then he shows us how to work the paddle. That's our training.

"Grasp the large vessel by the broad side. Hold it 10 centimeters above the smaller vessel. Tilt the large vessel so the beads fall into the smaller vessel. Do not shake the vessel. Now repeat the operation using the small vessel. Pour the beads into the larger vessel.

"Dip the paddle in the container with agitation. Stop the agitation. Withdraw the paddle at an angle of 37.5 degrees. Take the paddle with the beads to the inspectors. The paddle holds exactly 50 beads.

"The inspectors will silently and independently count the number of red beads.

"The chief inspector is responsible for the count. He will compare the count of the inspectors. He will announce the correct count. He then says, 'Dismissed!' The worker thereupon returns the beads to the large vessel".

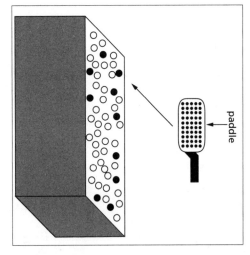

paddle

Dr. Deming places the paddle on the overhead projector and says,

"There are 50 holes in the paddle. Why are there 50 holes?" (Audience guesses.)

"There are 50 holes because there are 5 in one direction and 10 in the other." (Laughter)

Dr. Deming announces that we are on the Merit System. After every person had a turn he makes the following comments:

Day 1	
Mary	9
Bruce	7
Mike	12
Sue	7
Tony	8
Me	9
Total	52
Cumulative Average	8.7

"Bruce gets a merit increase."

"Mike gets probation."

"Sue gets a merit increase."

This looks easy enough. I can do pretty well. I sure don't want to get high defects in front of so many people.

Well, this looks simple enough, I didn't drop the paddle; that was good. I had only 9 red beads, 9 defects. Maybe I can get a better score next time.

I'm not sure of where this exercise is heading. I've heard about Dr. Deming's Red Bead Exercise, but there doesn't appear to be much to it.

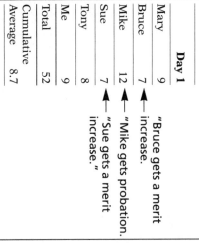

The Red Beads—Production—Day 2

Each dip of the paddle is a day's production for a single worker. The paddle has 50 holes and a bead goes into each hole. The red ones are defects and are easy to count. As we take our turns, Dr. Deming comments:

Well, they haven't noticed me yet; that's probably good. I wonder what Sue is doing. They haven't noticed that Tony is also doing pretty well. Do they shake the container less, or is it the way they hold

	Day 1	Day 2
Mary	9	8	← "Mary is improving."
Bruce	7	8
Mike	12	12	← "Mike is still on probation."
Sue	7	8	← "Sue is one of the best."
Tony	8	7
Me	9	10
Total	52	53
Cumulative Average	8.7	8.8

Dr. Deming says, "I thought when we gave people (Bruce and Sue) a merit raise they would try to do better to show they were worthy!!! But, the second day is worse than the first. The president wants a complete report."

My scores are nothing to get excited about. Compared to Mike, I look good. However, the others are doing better. I'm glad I have the last turn. Maybe I can learn something from the others. I don't want the foreman to yell at me. I think Bruce has a good technique. He aims for those areas in the container that show fewer red beads. That's what I am going to do next time my turn comes around. I'll only get a few seconds to aim the paddle. Still, with all the commotion, I'll have a chance. I know I can do better.

the paddle? I have decided to watch Sue and Tony. Poor Mike, he does look clumsy.

There is much laughter. Dr. Deming is making this demonstration into a joke. I don't want to look silly by getting a high score.

Dr. Deming is showing the people how to hold the paddle correctly. Hold it at a 37.5 degree angle.

The Red Beads—Production—Day 3

	Day 1	Day 2	Day 3
Mary	9	8	16
Bruce	7	8	14
Mike	12	12	7
Sue	7	8	13
Tony	8	7	5
Me	9	10	6
Total	52	53	61
Cumulative Average	8.7	8.8	9.2

Dr. Deming's comments:

"Halt the line. What is happening? The president wants a complete report. Why has performance gone down?"

"That's much better. Mike was on probation, but now he is doing better. Our progressive discipline really works."

"Sue just got careless. It happens sometimes after a merit raise. But I like her attitude and am sure she will get better."

One worker says "bad equipment." Yet it was the same equipment that we had in Day 1 and that day we were 15 percent better. In my company a 15 percent change in anything gets a lot of attention.

I know this is only a game. I certainly did better. What happened to Bruce? He got worse! And, what I don't understand is how Mike went from 12 defects to 7 defects. He got better fast. It doesn't appear to matter how many red beads Sue gets. Hmm, maybe this is more real than I thought.

The Red Beads—Production—Day 4

Dr. Deming reminds us at the start of production. "Remember: Work smarter not harder. Do it right the first time. Zero defects. Quality is up to you. Quality counts."

Wait a minute, I've used these same slogans! What good are they now? "Work smarter." Maybe I am really working smarter than anyone else. I got only 6 red beads last round. I am pleased even though I know this is only a game.

	Day 1	Day 2	Day 3	Day 4
Mary	9	8	16	6
Bruce	7	8	14	12
Mike	12	12	7	5
Sue	7	8	13	10
Tony	8	7	5	13
Me	9	10	6	6
Total	52	53	61	52
Cumulative Average	8.7	8.8	9.2	

Dr. Deming's comments:

"Better, but remember we want zero defects. The customers only pay for good products."

"Sue, better than yesterday. Yesterday she just got careless. That happens sometimes. After people get a merit increase, it goes to their heads." (Laughter)

"See, we gave Tony a merit increase and it went to his head."

Hey, I did great, I knew Mike was uncoordinated. Look, I got only 6 red beads. My technique paid off. I aimed the paddle and scored better. However, does this game make sense? It looks like Dr. Deming is trying to prove that it doesn't matter what the workers do, there will always be some red beads. The number jumps around. Could these just be random. Could they really random? Are they really random? I have used the word "random" before. Was I misusing the term? I am learning. Am I really doing better than everyone else? I thought that was the case, but now I am not so sure. I'm not going to speak up in front of all these people.

Keeping the Plant Open with the Best Workers

Now Dr. Deming says: "We are going to keep the factory open with our best workers. This is our contribution to management theory. The record is very clear on who are the best."

This reminds me of when we downsized my company. It was tough to decide who would go and who would stay. As managers, we spent countless hours on these decisions. We operated under the theory that it was management's job to make these tough decisions.

We prided ourselves on how diligent we were to face these tough decisions. I'm getting a bit uncomfortable recognizing that I have made so many naive decisions. Were all of our decisions based on random variation and not on the differences in performance we thought existed? Could that have been the reason our profits declined?

	Day 1	Day 2	Day 3	Day 4	Total	
Mary	9	8	16	6	39	← Fired
Bruce	7	8	14	12	41	← Fired
Mike	12	12	7	5	36	
Sue	7	8	13	10	38	← Fired
Tony	8	7	5	13	33	
Me	9	10	6	6	31	
Total	52	53	61	52	218	
Cumulative Average	8.7	8.8	9.2	9.1	9.1	

Dr. Deming continues, "Using only the best workers, we will keep production going."

So instead of six workers, he keeps only three, based on their productivity. Mary, Bruce, and Sue are laid off. That is fair enough.

It was a surprise to see Bruce and Sue gone. Sue was one of the best operators according to the foreman. Bruce invented the method that got me low scores. What happened?

Mike's performance was a big surprise also. Maybe he pulled himself together. Now let's see if I can win this game.

The Red Beads—Production—Day 5

Only three workers remain on day 5. We each work two shifts to produce the 300 total beads required per day. In a real job, we would be exhausted by the time the second shift started, just like the overtime we work so frequently.

Oh, no. Look at the first results. I got 14 red beads. Why didn't my system work this time? I did the same action as before, aiming for an area with fewer red beads. Is this game just dumb luck? Is no skill involved?

Mike was the worst of the remaining operators (36 defects), but this time around he got only 7 red beads. How did he get so low a score? Let's wait until the second shift. Then we will see what is what.

We proceeded with the second shift. Mike still had the low score. When we added the two shift scores together we were unhappy.

In fact our overall quality (66) was worse than any previous day's production. Tony and I had worse results than Mike. How can that be? It is no trick to identify the best workers in the past. Just look at the numbers. However, doing that is no guarantee that they will perform that way in the future.

This idea of defects being random events is troubling. This exercise was very much like the working world. I've always

believed that the workers made defects. This simulation shows that, regardless what people do, the errors just appear.

Thank goodness it is soon lunch. I have to think this over.

	Day 1	Day 2	Day 3	Day 4	Total	Day 5 A.M.	Day 5 P.M.
Mary	9	8	16	6	39		
Bruce	7	8	14	12	41		
Mike	12	12	7	5	36	7	
Sue	7	8	13	10	38		
Tony	8	7	5	13	33	12	
Me	9	10	6	6	31	14	
Total	52	53	61	52	218	Total =	
Cumulative Average	8.7	8.8	9.2	9.1	9.1		

	Day 1	Day 2	Day 3	Day 4	Total	Day 5 A.M.	Day 5 P.M.
Mary	9	8	16	6	39		
Bruce	7	8	14	12	41		
Mike	12	12	7	5	36	7	9
Sue	7	8	13	10	38		
Tony	8	7	5	13	33	12	13
Me	9	10	6	6	31	14	11
Total	52	53	61	52	218	Total =	66
Cumulative Average	8.7	8.8	9.2	9.1	9.1		

The Red Beads

Red Beads Chart

To examine the activities in the Red Bead exercise, construct a Control Chart. The data in the exercise were in the form of attributes; the beads were either red or white (= not red). The beads had the attribute of red or did not have it. It counted as "1" if the attribute was present in a bead. It counted as "0" if the attribute was absent. The inspectors added the 0's and 1's recorded for each sample of 50 items drawn by the willing workers.

In twenty-four (6 workers × 4 days) drawings a total of 218 red beads occurred. The average number of red beads was

	Day 1	Day 2	Day 3	Day 4	Total
Mary	9	8	16	6	39
Bruce	7	8	14	12	41
Mike	12	12	7	5	36
Sue	7	8	13	10	38
Tony	8	7	5	13	33
Me	9	10	6	6	31
Total	52	53	61	52	218
Cumulative Average	8.7	8.8	9.2	9.1	9.1

$$\bar{x} = \frac{\Sigma \text{Red Beads}}{\text{Number of Trials}} = \frac{218}{24} = 9.08 \text{ or } 9.1$$

The uppercase Greek letter Σ [reads "sigma"] means "sum of."

The average percentage of red beads is given by

$$\bar{p} = \frac{\Sigma \text{Red Beads}}{\text{Number of Trials} \times \text{Beads per Trial}} = \frac{218}{24 \times 50} = .1817$$

To compute the control limits for a chart of this type, we use the formula

$$\text{UCL}_{\rangle} = \bar{x} \pm 3 \times \sqrt{\bar{x} \times (1 - \bar{p})}$$

$$\text{LCL}_{\rangle}$$

$$= 9.08 \pm 3 \times \sqrt{9.08 \times (1 - .1817)}$$
$$= 9.08 \pm 3 \times 2.7258$$
$$= 9.08 \pm 8.18$$

Therefore, the upper control limit (UCL) is

$$\text{UCL} = 9.08 + 8.18 = 17.26 \cong 17$$

and the Lower Control limit (LCL) is

$$\text{LCL} = 9.08 - 8.18 = 0.90 \cong 1$$

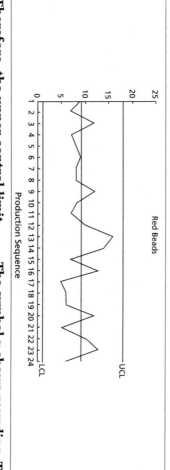

Red Beads

The symbol $\cong$ shows rounding. The additional places are not material in plotting the data. The plot above shows that the process was random. All the variation came from common causes.

The Light Goes On

Now I got it. The whole red bead experiment was a big game. I took the bait, I believed the boss. I actually thought that by concentrating, by being smart, by thinking, I could earn a lower defect rate. The role play opened my eyes.

Now it is clear. Sure the numbers jumped around, up and down. Those were just random fluctuations. I attached meaning to random fluctuations! When my defect rate dropped from 10 red beads to 6 red beads, I thought it was due to something I personally did, the way I aimed the paddle.

Sure, I had knowledge of my score. I had knowledge of my technique. I thought I gained knowledge from watching other workers. Until this moment, however, I didn't know the meaning of "Profound Knowledge."

Now I begin to grasp the concept. I was a willing worker in a system. The system consisted of the vessels, paddle, red beads, white beads, instructions, and procedures. Just like the real workplace. The environment, equipment, materials, and procedures are all designed by management. The willing worker arrives ready to work. The worker then becomes part of a system.

Then the Theory of Variation comes into play. Of course the numbers went up and down. However, these differences were random. When drawn on a control chart with calculated control limits, even I could see the pattern of variation. The numbers changed, but the changes were not significant. In reacting to these chance changes with psychological prizes, such as merit raises, we were creating superstitious learning.

Just because I got only 6 defects (red beads), I actually believed in my heart that my technique of aiming the paddle made a difference. I developed a hypothesis that I could successfully aim the paddle, and I would get a 6. Then I aimed again and I scored another low (6) defect rate. That convinced me even more that I had, through my best efforts, improved performance. Then management announced that they were laying off the other workers and keeping me as one of the best performers. In my secret mind I reveled in my own personal glory of conquest, I beat Mary, Sue, and Bruce. I felt a personal victory, just like the psychological glow I feel at work when I outdo my co-workers. I won the game.

With disciplined concentration (best efforts), I aimed the paddle as before and in my final two trials I got 14 and 11! So much for my theory of aiming the paddle. Drawing the control chart, I realized that best efforts drew me down an erroneous path, one that I had traveled many times before.

Day Two—Afternoon

We return from lunch. The morning has been fun. There was much laughing during the red bead exercise. Although I laughed at the silliness of the mock workplace, it was startlingly real. Dr. Deming is proving to us that the numbers we look at in the workplace are not as trustworthy as we thought. This is very troubling.

Back at my company, I spend hours and hours looking at numbers. We make large investments based upon numbers. We use numbers to decide whom to fire, promote, or transfer. The Japanese credit Dr. Deming with their economic recovery. Here he is telling me that the way my company looks at numbers is wrong.

He is actually saying that we are wrong. He is not equivocating, saying that we could do it better or that we are missing the mark. He is saying that we do damage with our current practices.

It is good that this seminar lasts for four days. I will need this time to absorb all the new concepts and figure out how they impact my company. These new ideas make sense. However, I have been doing many things differently from what Dr. Deming recommends. I have been successful. I get the feeling that using his methods would have made me much more successful. Have I been missing the boat? I am getting the impression there is much more to learn.

I recall a passage about the Walker spy ring (John Walker sold top secret codes and drawings for making code reading machines to the Soviet Union): "So much didn't make sense over the past ten years. So many times the Russians and the Vietnamese [knew] what we were going to do. Only later did we learn our secret ciphers were . . . regularly read."[1] Walker may have caused massive losses of unknowable proportions. Could our misunderstanding of variation in America have caused the loss of thousands of manufacturing jobs?

Could our reliance on numbers be so wrong? Dr. Deming is telling us to understand variation. The way he looks at numbers is different from the way I do. I look at everything as though it were absolute. Dr. Deming understands that results have variation. He looks at numbers to manage processes. I look at numbers to manage results. I have to change.

Each day at work I get numbers from our Management Information System. We've spent millions of dollars on this system. Our top people developed this system. We had the foremost consultants that money could buy. Yet, from the red bead game, I see that these reports are only recording a series of random events. They are just measuring dumb luck.

Could our MIS be just measuring random events? Let me see. I've got a report here. Maybe during one of the breaks I could show it to the helper who is assisting Dr. Deming . . . .

[1] Early, Pete. *Family of Spies*. New York: Bantam Books 1988, p. 11.

It Is So Easy to Be Fooled by Figures

Dr. Deming reminds us that in our demonstration we gave merit raises and put people on probation. Yet all the errors were part of the system's performance, not the individual worker's.

Dr. Deming says that we have acted as though the number of red beads came entirely from the workers. We neglected the impact of the system. He then draws the following equation on the overhead projector:

X + [XY] = Red Beads

Where X is the worker effect, Y is the system effect (see page 123).

	Day 1	Day 2	Day 3	Day 4	Total
Mary	9	8	16	6	39
Bruce	7	8	14	12	41
Mike	12	12	7	5	36
Sue	7	8	13	10	38
Tony	8	7	5	13	33
Me	9	10	6	6	31
Total	52	53	61	52	218
Cumulative Average	8.7	8.8	9.2	9.1	

Dr. Deming goes on to say, "We have here an equation with two unknowns. He who can solve a single equation with two unknowns is entitled to judge people." (Laughter)

I remember that in high school algebra I learned that it takes two equations to solve for two unknowns. Am I guilty of doing this? Now that I think about it, yes. I promoted Roger over Henry based on their sales figures. Now I know why I have regretted that decision ever since.

Dr. Deming feels that the workers contribute at most 6 percent to the

problems that occur. Ninety-four percent of the problems come from the system. Yet most efforts at improvement have been aimed at the worker.

"The worker is not the problem. The system is the problem. If you want to improve performance you must work on the system."

What does he mean by "work on the system?" Isn't that what I do each day, all day, look at all of the problems? Have I got my priorities wrong? I have to concentrate on the system, not the problems if I want to get improvement in my company.

Dr. Deming continues: "When does it pay to look for something? When should we leave our system alone? You must have a theory. You need to know why you are looking at numbers, what you are trying to accomplish."

Referring to the table shown on this page, Dr. Deming says, "You will all do your own chart tonight. It will take you two hours."

Dr. Deming expects everyone to do the chart for the bead experiment. The reader is invited to do the same as an exercise.

What Can We Do to Reduce the Proportion of Red Beads

One job of management is to use numbers to predict the future.

Each prediction is an experiment. If we can predict the future we can predict costs and quality. We will know how many beads we need to produce a certain outcome.

Contrast this to the chaos when we can predict nothing.

The red beads trouble me. It is clear that to reduce the number of red beads in the paddle we must remove them from the container.

Dr. Deming elaborates, "Management should be working with the supplier to reduce the number of red beads. Reduce the lot-by-lot variation. That is how to get better numbers.

"In one session one of the workers tried to bribe an inspector with a dollar!!! (Laughter) People will risk breaking the rules to get better numbers.

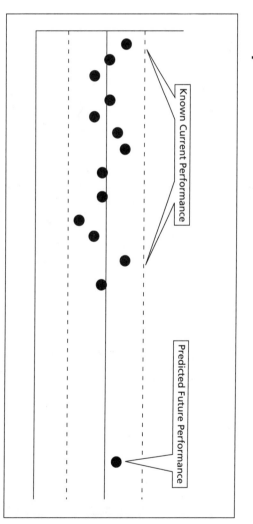

Known Current Performance

Predicted Future Performance

"What is the purpose of management? Not to play games but to use numbers so we can plan and predict the future."

· **If we know the control limits and our system is stable we can predict future performance with some certainty. We won't be right every time. There is some risk, we can't predict too far in advance but we can predict.**

Charts should be long and narrow. One requires only one to three inches in height. Charts are for analytic purposes, not engineering drawings.

How Did This Come About

Dr. Deming tells the story of Dr. Shewhart's work: "In 1925 I was at the Hawthorne Plant of Western Electric. People were already talking about the work of Dr. Shewhart. I did not meet him until 1927.

"I reported on the first morning to Mr. Chester M. Coulter. Mr. Coulter exacted out of me straightaway a promise not to get caught on the stairways when the whistle blows. The women will trample you to death with their heels as they run out of the plant and there would be no record! (Laughter)

"In 1925 they were trying to get uniformity of product. They advertised, 'As alike as two telephones.' They were mass producing phones and consistency was critical. Every time something went wrong management investigated the problem. They corrected all problems they saw. Matters just got worse. You make matters worse by everyone just doing his best!!! (Audience laughs)

"They turned to Dr. Walter Shewhart at Bell Labs. Dr. Shewhart helped them out."

Dr. Shewhart faced the problem of when to stop the production line and when to let it continue to operate. If he stopped the line on the basis of a sample and there were only good telephones on the line, he made a mistake. On the other hand, if he did not stop the line and there were bad telephones produced, he made a mistake. See the next page for further treatment of this dilemma.

Note: The title of Dr. Shewhart's 1931 pioneering work is *The Economic Control of Quality of Manufactured Product*. Dr. Shewhart's contribution came at a critical moment of the Industrial Revolution. Dr. Deming invited Dr. Shewhart to lecture at the Department of Agriculture in 1939. Dr. Deming edited Dr. Shewhart's lecture notes and published them as *Statistical Methods from the Viewpoint of Quality Control*. Later Dr. Deming wrote an eloquent foreword to Shewhart's first book when the American Society for Quality Control republished this work. Until the 1980s, mainstream American management overlooked both classic books. Both books are again in print.

Two Kinds of Mistakes

> Mistake 1. To react to an outcome as if it came from a special cause when actually it came from common causes of variation.
>
> Mistake 2. To treat an outcome as if it came from common causes of variation, when it actually came from a special cause.

Mistake 1 is stopping the production line on the basis of a sample when there are only good telephones on it. Mistake 2 is failing to stop the line on the basis of a sample even though bad telephones exist.

Dr. Shewhart recognized that one can avoid mistake 1 completely. Simply never stop the line. If one opts never to make mistake 1, they will commit mistake 2 a maximum of times. The same holds true when avoiding mistake 2 all the time.

Dr. Shewhart recognized that mistake 1 or 2 occurs from time to time. He directed his research to minimizing the economic loss of making one

or the other mistake from time to time. The outcome of his experiments resulted in the "Control Chart." By experimenting, he found the most economic decision exists when using the average plus or minus three standard deviations.

Shewhart theorized that every system has infinite sources of variation. We need a method to help us judge

which fluctuations come from the endless source of random causes and which come from special causes of variation. A control chart is an operational definition of special causes. Dr. Shewhart used the term "assignable causes."

Dr. Deming asks, "When do you look for a special cause?" He answers, "When a point falls outside the control limits."

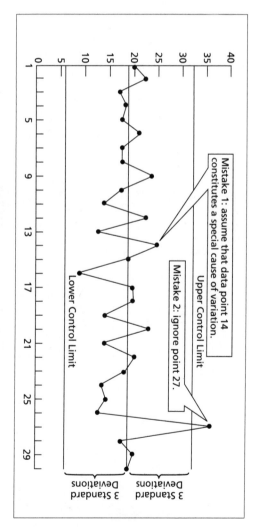

How Do You Make Red Beads

"How many beads were there in the bead box?

"By census count, years ago when I set up the exercise, there were:

Beads	Count	Percent
Total	4,000	100
Red	800	20
White	3,200	80

In 1920 Professor Wilbur Hitchcock taught variation by making each student make 10 blocks of cement. Dr. Deming said, "I learned variation myself by actually mixing cement. Then I crushed the cement and analyzed the content. They were all different. That even surprised me!!! (Laughter)

"Any chemist can tell you that paint pigments are different. They feel different. They feel different to the paddle. How do we make red beads? We buy them white. Take them home. Dip them in pigment. Lay them out to dry. Give them a second coat."

Over the years I have used different paddles. Here are data on each:

Paddle #	Average Red Beads
1	11.3
2	9.6
3	9.2
4	9.4

"Imagine you were buying coal by the ton. Paying for a carbon content of 11.3 and receiving coal that has a carbon content of only 9.2"

Dr. Deming raises an interesting point. I was very curious when he drew the run chart and showed that the average number of red beads was 9.1. Why wasn't it 10? Twenty percent of the beads in the material are red. The paddle holds 50 beads. Twenty percent of 50 is 10. Dr. Deming said that the bead process was mechanical. In mechanical sampling, factors other than the material influence the outcome. I remember seeing in Mr. Scherkenbach's book that in addition to material, the

method, the people, the environment, and the equipment influence the outcome.[1] That is the reason why over the long run each paddle gives a different number of red beads. They are different pieces of equipment. This is important in our business.

Then Dr. Deming mentions the point about the coal, then everything makes more sense. These very small differences can make a big difference in the work world.

[1] William W. Scherkenbach, *The Deming Route*, Chapter 3.

Blank Beads	→	Dip in white paint	→	Dry	→	Dip in red paint	→	Dry

As a Result of the Red Bead Experiment the Japanese Went to Work Straight Away

Yawata Steel Company
22 December 1955

The Estimation of Iron (Fe) Content

Ore	Class	Old Method	New Method	Difference
Dungun	A	59.95	55.33	4.62
Larap	B	56.60	55.30	1.30
Larap	C	59.25	58.06	1.19
Samar	D	55.55	50.42	5.13

The method in effect in 1950 was to take the sample from the ship. Since iron ore is heavy, the chances were good that the sample came from the top of the pile.

The study team under Dr. Ishikawa used a new method of sampling the ore during unloading. Two lines showed the sample location. At random intervals, they halted the conveyor. At each halt the ore between the lines became the sample.

The change in method gave a very different result. The table shows the difference.

Dr. Deming noted that you cannot find the Yawata Steel plant any more. It long ago merged with the Fuji Steel plant to become today's Nippon Steel.

Dr. Deming tells the story of how Dr. Kaoru Ishikawa began to study the method of getting a sample of iron ore. The ore came from a ship delivering it to the Yawata Steel Company. Dr. Deming's eight-day course in 1950 used the bead experiment. The Japanese began to wonder if the sampling method for iron ore was what they should use. The red bead exercise had much in common with the sampling method. Both were mechanical sampling.

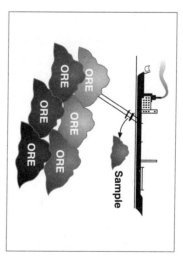

Sample

I Am Learning

Dr. Deming raises basic questions. He says we have been living on wealth from natural resources. He warns that it won't last forever. Without a change we will not make it. We need to look at new ways to understand our system. If we understand the theory of variation we know that it is futile to ask for something outside the system's capability.

One of my friends is the Chief Executive Officer of a small company. The performance of the Chicago Region was poor. For three years running this region produced only 7.5 million dollars of sales per year. My friend needed 10 million dollars to make keeping the office open a viable matter. "A fact of life," as Dr. Deming says. The chart showed a steady state, flat sales.

From what I learned today, sales is a system. If the system is stable, then managers must apply leadership to change to a new level of performance. For the past three years my friend simply raised the sales quotas and gave pep talks. He must make a basic change.

I am beginning to catch on to the theory of variation and psychology.

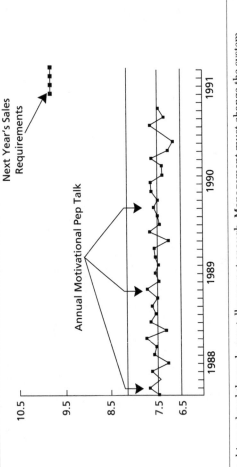

Next Year's Sales Requirements

Annual Motivational Pep Talk

To achieve a breakthrough, pep talks are not enough. Management must change the system.

At my company we decide what to do by looking at financial numbers. We look for exceptions. I see that the financial data is not enough.

We look at which worker has the highest error rate and then we take corrective action. Or we look to see if the percent of errors has gone up or down. If it goes up, we call everyone together for a meeting. In the meeting, we "motivate them" to do better, and usually that works for a while.

When the errors go down we give a bonus, or maybe we will have a pizza party. Dr. Deming is saying this is wrong—even worse, it is destructive. He warns us,

"Do not export American management to a friendly country." How right he is.

6

Obligations 10 through 14

Obligation 10—Eliminate Slogans, Exhortations, Arbitrary Targets

D r. Deming says: "It is all right to show what management is thinking, but slogans are an insult . . ."

Dr. Deming explains: "How can a person do it right the first time if he knows not what to do? If he has not been trained, or if the training was rushed, or if his tools are shoddy, or his incoming materials are off-gauge . . ."

At my company we have lots of slogans. We print up wall posters that remind everyone of our zero defect program. We have a new slogan every month. We get colorful posters with cute cartoons. I used to think that these are just helpful reminders. Now I can see that a slogan like "Do it right the first time" is at best useless and at worst dangerous.

If we have set up our business correctly, it will be done right the first time. In that case the slogan is useless.

If we did not set it up correctly, there is nothing that the worker can do to make it right the first time. If we didn't set up the business properly, a slogan such as this will only frustrate the worker. If the

worker tries to make changes, he can only make the result worse by tampering.

"Exhortations and posters generate frustration and resentment. They advertise to the production worker that management is unaware of barriers to pride of workmanship . . ."

> **Do it right the first time.**
> **Be a quality worker.**
> **Take pride in your work.**
> **Think**

Why Do Exhortations and Arbitrary Targets Create Frustration

Dr. Deming continues, "Management sets a goal and posts it for all to see. Isn't that good?"

Is this just a motivational issue? Or does it go deeper?

Dr. Deming tells how he came to a plant where management posted, in the cafeteria, a big chart for all to see. See the replica of the charts on this page. Both charts show a stable system. Goal lines originally drawn in red appear on both charts. The chart for production shows improvement. It also shows a new goal line. The improvement came about by the installation of a new machine. Industrial engineers computed the arbitrary goal lines.

As the system is stable, the responsibility for improvement rests with management, the controller of the system. If the workers tried to make change, they can only tamper with the system. This will make the system worse.

Oh!! Now I get it. We ask our people to perform at a level that is beyond the capability of our systems. That's like the red beads. We are asking workers to avoid red beads, but only management can remove

the beads. We are asking people to do what they cannot. And when we use slogans, that is just adding fuel to the flame.

We set goals without ever dealing with the ideas of a control chart. We just look

at the best previous point and add some percentage points to it. If we fulfill the goal, we just up it again.

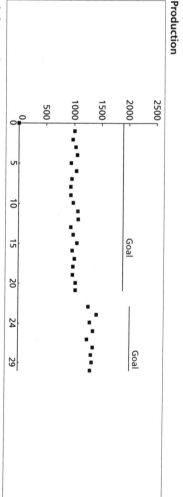

Proportion Defective

This system is stable and goal cannot be reached.

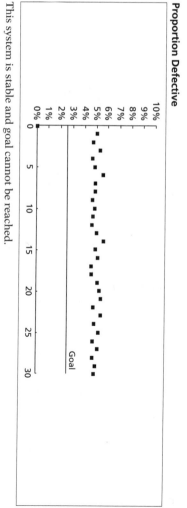

Production

Shift in performance is due to management's purchase of new machine.

Obligation 11—Eliminate Numerical Quotas for the Workforce

Dr. Deming tells of a woman in his class at New York University. She told him about her job at an airline. She answered the phones, made reservations, and gave information. Management set her the goals of twenty-five calls per hour and being courteous. Computer breakdowns and slowdowns plagued her. Often she had to use time-consuming manual directories. Her dilemma: to make the quota of twenty-five calls or give courteous service? How can one do both?

What would I do in her situation? I would concentrate on making the twenty-five call quota because no one would really know if I am courteous. Management will judge me on that which they measure with ease.

Why use quotas? I learned in business school that people work best under pressure. Frederick W. Taylor said that workers will not do their job unless management drives them continuously. Taylor used the word "soldiering." It made sense at the time. We developed management systems of rewards and punishments to motivate our people. We devote much of our time as managers and much of our overhead to running quotas.

We spent a lot of effort on developing payment schedules for those who met their quotas. As I moved up the corporate ladder I learned many creative ways to make my quota. Usually I was careful not to exceed my quota by too much. If I figured out a way to make an improvement, I would keep it to myself.

The whole quota scheme was and still is an elaborate game we all play to pretend we are making matters better. We base it upon the assumption that the individual has full control over the process. From the red bead exercise I realize this is not so.

What is my job?

To take twenty-five calls per hour?

OR

To give callers courteous satisfaction?

An airline job:
- **Answer telephone**
- **Twenty-five calls per hour**
- **Be courteous**
- **Don't rush callers**

Incentives Are Quotas

This reminds me of my friend who owns a trucking company. He put his warehouse people on an incentive program. He and his management team spent weeks thinking of how to run the incentive program. What happened? After a few weeks, his damaged goods increased. They came up with the idea of a bonus when damage was zero. This appeared to do the job in the short run. Any damage would ruin the bonus for that reporting period. Once they lost the bonus, people did not care if they created more damage. They had to work faster to make up for the lost bonus.

Meanwhile, the entire incentive and bonus system was becoming a monster to administer. Now I can see why my friend, with the best of intentions, with expert help, was merely tampering, making matters worse.

My friend did not have the benefit of Profound Knowledge. Management's job is not just to mandate quotas, but to examine the system of production. This is so whether the system is material handling or information handling.

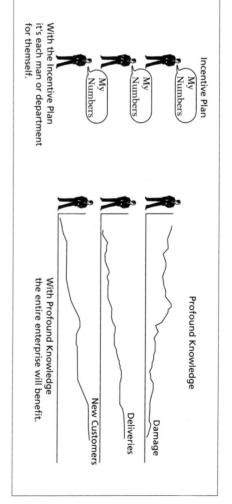

Incentive Plan

My Numbers / My Numbers / My Numbers

With the Incentive Plan it's each man or department for themself.

Profound Knowledge

Damage / Deliveries / New Customers

With Profound Knowledge the entire enterprise will benefit.

My friend relied on incentives to raise productivity. In consequence, management did no further work on process improvement. The onus for productivity was on the worker. In an adversary environment of quotas, the workers have no

incentive to help management. They keep any improvement they find to themselves. They are also afraid to produce more. They fear that management will raise the quota if they show greater production is possible.

What About a Person Who Doesn't Give a Hoot?

Dr. Deming, in a quiet, thoughtful voice, tells the story about a professor at New York University who " . . . did nothing. Yes, he taught, he drew his pay, but he made no contribution. He stopped caring. He stopped learning, he stopped contributing . . .

"Then two fine men asked him to contribute to their book. He imparted knowledge. They gave him a chance, appreciating the knowledge that he had. He changed, he grew, and he started to contribute."

We had an office in California with a demoralized staff. The morale was lowest, productivity was lowest; in almost every measurement they were at bottom. Certainly, it was a situation in which "no one gave a hoot."

The manager went to a lecture by one of Dr. Deming's proteges. Returning with a new understanding of management's job, she rethought her own job. In the past, she had acted as a policewoman who inspected and controlled our MBO's and quotas. On return from the training, she interviewed our staff to learn what barriers they faced in doing their jobs. She

found faulty equipment, poor training, lack of common definitions, all matters for which management is responsible.

She changed her thinking from being a controller to being a leader. She personally started to lead improvement efforts. Her office went from the worst to being on top. She made improvements, based upon sound theories, and shared these with others. Her efforts led to improvements everywhere.

She truly proved that a good leader can convert people who "don't give a hoot."

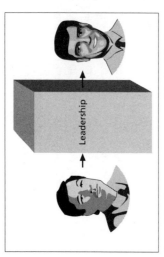

A good leader can convert people who "don't give a hoot" into effective employees.

Obligations 10 through 14

How to Survive When the Company Insists on a Quota

As I listen to Dr. Deming, I remember a family crisis.

Dad arrives home, we sit at the dinner table and we all sense something is wrong. Dad is a hardware salesman, he represents several out-of-town factories, selling their goods to wholesalers in the New York City market.

Tonight, uncommonly, something upset Dad. He explains that his biggest account has just gone to a computerized quota system. For each account that is lower from last quarter to this quarter he must send an explanation to the factory president. Dad and Mom sit at the kitchen table and make up explanation after explanation.

A year later Dad mentions, in passing, that he rarely needs such explanations anymore. He has figured out how to inch his sales up each quarter so there is almost always some level of improvement. Occasionally, he will under-order, even build up an inventory so the numbers look good at quarterly report.

This was his way of telling me not to worry, the crisis is over, the family is safe.

In later years he took me into the business during the summers. He practiced many of the principles that Dr. Deming proposes. I always sensed that he understood that he was part of a larger system. He understood and watched the marketplace so he could adjust to the future. When tract housing became popular he had a line of folding closet doors. When home security became the vogue he planned by getting a line of chain door guards and security locks.

His system was in control, it was stable. Long-term business relationships based upon trust were his hallmark.

Alternatives to Quotas—Change from MBO to MBP

Dr. Deming's voice picks up volume, "My church newsletter announces a goal—we will increase our membership. By what method? The Department of Education announces schools will be better by the year 2000. They issue a report full of goals such as every adult will be literate. **By what method?** High school graduation rate will increase to at least 90 percent. **By what method?"**

Dr. Deming has a way of using his voice when he wants to drive home a point. His voice is like that of a singer, and he gets our attention. I'm beginning to get the message. When we give a quota or goal without an in-depth look at the plan for achieving it, we are really not managing. In fact, we may actually be making matters worse.

Management by Objectives (MBO) has become an adversary game in which we just focus on results. Management of results has hazards. People operating under MBO will perform only enough to look good to their supervisor. They will avoid doing

more. If they greatly exceed targets set for them, MBO requires a raise in next year's targets. Workers understand variation better than their managers. They know that results will vary up or down from one measurement to the next. They want to keep their quota as low as possible. In effect, MBO sets a ceiling on performance.

A salesman selling more than his quota will bank some orders to help next month's quota. The damage to plant scheduling is unknown.

In running a business we have to attain certain levels of performance to stay viable as a business. Dr. Deming calls such numbers "facts of life." Examples of these are targets for sales, quality, and similar performance numbers needed for corporate survival. Announcing these numbers, posting them, stamping our feet, or pounding the table does nothing to achieve the numbers. What we need is a plan for how to achieve these numbers: the method.

If Management by Objectives does not serve a useful purpose, what can I, as a manager, do?

The answer is Management by Planning (MBP). This focuses on process, not outcome. Instead of just negotiating quotas, we need to work with our people to create a plan.

We will use what machinery, what manpower, what material, and what methods? As CEO, I have an aim (fact of life). Instead of "negotiating" an MBO with each of my people I will use an alternative. We sit down together and develop a plan to meet our aims. I don't want my people playing numbers games with me, holding back sales and production so they can manage their quotas. Instead I want to manage by planning.

If each department optimizes their own MBO, their own set of numbers, then the whole company might suffer. Sometimes one department must give something up so the whole company can succeed.

Obligation 12A—Remove Barriers to Pride of Workmanship

Dr. Deming inquires: "How can anyone have pride in workmanship when he must produce defective goods?" He pauses, looks at his notes, then continues, ". . . some say it comes from failure to communicate." He tells the story of a worker who stops his machine for adjustment. The foreman, seeing this, insists the worker get back to production immediately. Never mind the adjustment, just run it. The worker knows that this will produce defective items. The foreman knows it also. There is no failure to communicate. Dr. Deming said to the worker, "You understood what the foreman said, didn't you?" The worker's reply was, "He ordered me to make defective items. Where is my pride of workmanship?"

With only a moment's hesitation Dr. Deming drives the point home again. He tells of a woman who spends too much time replacing tools. She says that cutting tools are soft and of low quality. Dr. Deming asks: "But the company saves money by buying cheap tools?" She replies that the company loses ten times what they save because of worn-out tools and lost time.

His voice raises in tempo: "A woman protests she must wait for a technician when her machine goes down. 'Why object, you get paid for waiting?' Money could not pay me for the stress I endure waiting for that man to come."

His gentle sarcasm is biting. "Why protest, you get paid for waiting?" That is just how we, as managers, believe our employees think. We think they have no pride in workmanship. We think they have no loyalty for company. We care little for them. They in turn care little for us.

How is it that new employees come to a company with enthusiasm, readiness and willingness to work, happy? Yet within a week they are just like all other employees. Some companies are expert at destroying pride of workmanship.

A friend, who owns a machine shop, interviewed his workers. He describes how surprised he was to learn that a lack of tools terribly upset his people. How could they do good work if the tools from the crib were either defective or not available? Skilled workers like to take pride in their

"Why protest, you get paid for waiting?"

"Money would not pay me for the stress I endure..."

work. Not having the tools with which to do the job frustrates them.

My friend bought more tools. The positive impact on morale was unmeasurable. Dr. Deming likes to quote Dr. Nelson, "The most important problems of management are unknown and unknowable."

Obligation 12B—Drop the Annual Merit Review

Appraisal Day

> I hate to
> give appraisals

> I hate to
> take appraisals

Appraisals and merit reviews prevent workers from having pride of workmanship. **We suppose that the use of the annual merit review gets the best from workers. As Dr. Deming says, "The result is precisely the opposite. You get the worst out of people. You don't get what you pay for."**

Appraisals create fear, reduce cooperation between workers (and managers), and focus on visible results only. **Frequently managers use appraisals as a salary administration tool. They use them to reward and punish. Appraisals are subjective. They commonly do not reflect the actual performance or potential of the appraised person. Appraisals are a lie.**

In my company, we use annual appraisals. We rate people on a long list of topics. We score each of these from one through five. One is terrible and five is outstanding. Three is average. If I gave a three to any of my managers, he or she would quit. Yet three is supposedly normal performance. If I give a three to a manager in my company, the personnel

rule is that he cannot have a salary increase. No wonder they quit. This system has been in place before I came to the company. It is time we uprooted it.

My managers are going to have to learn to lead their people. It requires that managers understand their people. It requires that they develop them so the whole company improves. They will have to learn to help people. They must learn to use statistical methods to determine who needs special attention.

Why should we wait a full year for the annual appraisal to find out that a particular person needs help? A major task for my managers is to develop their people. Their job is to get them to become consistently good performers. That alone will increase the level of company-wide performance of my firm.

I know that many firms have changed and abolished their appraisal system. The results have in all cases borne out the contention that appraisals are destroying Western industry. Reading in Bill Scherkenbach's books I found some references to these successes.[1]

[1]Scherkenbach, W. W., *The Deming Route* (Washington, DC: CEEPress, 1986) Chapter 5 and Scherkenbach, W. W., *"Deming's Road to Continual Improvement"* (Knoxville, TN: SPC Press, 1991) pp. 292–293.

Obligation 13—Education and Growth

Dr. Deming proceeds: "Obligation 13 is about elevating people's minds. In any profession, good ones are hard to find so make good ones."

Dr. Deming's Obligation 6 deals with skill training for a specific job. Obligation 13 is also about learning. It is of a more general nature, something I can do voluntarily if it fits with my desires. Some years my family takes precedence, and I don't want to go to night school; other years I want to learn, to grow. I sense that Dr. Deming has a love of learning and wants to share that joy.

I wonder how our corporate culture handles the idea of lifelong learning. Do we encourage people, formally or informally, to study if they wish to enrich themselves? I wonder how many people we discourage from schooling because we send them on business trips. How many do we discourage by switching their shift schedules from day to evening?

I must find out who in my company is taking courses on his or her own time. I wish to make sure that their managers are supportive.

Dr. Deming describes a conversation from many years ago (1928). As he was leaving Hawthorne Plant of the Western Electric Company (today part of AT&T) to study for his Ph.D., his manager talked to him. The manager told him there would be a job waiting for him at the company when he completed his studies. They would pay him $9,000 a year. "I had heard there were people making that kind of money but I never expected to be one of them." His manager explained to him that the reason was they felt that he would be worth far more in the future.

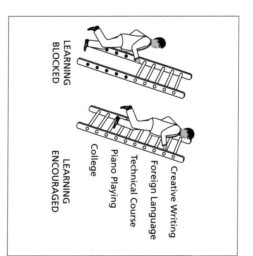

LEARNING
BLOCKED

LEARNING
ENCOURAGED

Creative Writing
Foreign Language
Technical Course
Piano Playing
College

Obligation 14A—Take Action to Accomplish the Transformation

I'm learning principles, concepts, and theories. I'm learning why to change, new ways of thinking. I want Dr. Deming to tell me exactly what to do. It would be so easy if he was like other consultants who recommend a cookbook approach. Do this, do that, one size fits all.

Dr. Deming is demanding more of me. He is demanding that I think. Rather than giving me a cookbook he is giving me a theory. Something I must think through. Something I must create. He is forcing me to be a leader, to step out in front, take a risk.

Well, let me see, how can I get started in my world? One approach is to hire a consultant, leave it all in his hands. If it works well, I can take credit. If it fails, he insulates me. Then I can fire the consultant. We pay them well; they can afford to take the hit.

Or I could appoint someone in my organization as a Quality Coordinator. That will get me off the hook and out of the direct line. I make that person report directly to me. Then it would sure look like I have interest in the process. I could pick a high-performing staff person, or even better yet pick a high-level executive, someone who has real power and authority.

This is nonsense. I am the one responsible for quality. I don't want to delegate. What I need is help.

I need a master consultant to work with me to help me think it through. I need a top-level person to become our own internal source of Profound Knowledge. However, and most important, I need to learn this body of knowledge myself. Then I can apply what I learn and deploy my knowledge to the next levels of the company.

Obligation 14B—An Example (Caution—Do Not Use Without Theory)

The CEO of the bank that I use hired one of Dr. Deming's helpers to work with him on a long-term basis. He studied under this master. Only when he felt comfortable with the concepts did he proceed. He asked his six bank presidents to attend a two-day session with the master. They discussed the concept as applied to the bank. The presidents got answers. Then the CEO asked if they wanted to continue to transform the bank along with Dr. Deming's principles. They agreed with enthusiasm.

The group then decided to hold similar sessions with senior and middle-level management. The CEO and presidents attended every session. The CEO asked each group if they had reservations or wanted to proceed. Each officer sent a confidential memorandum to the CEO whom they trusted. All but one agreed to continuing the process.

At this point, the CEO felt that he had reached a critical mass of support. However, he wanted one more group to support the effort. They held another session for the bank's board of directors.

When they became enthusiastic about the change, the actual process started.

The CEO offered a young, talented executive the opportunity to help the CEO in handling the details of transformation. This executive worked with the master and the CEO.

As a first step, the CEO, the executive, and the presidents set about reexamining the aims of the bank. Based on the principles that they had learned, they developed an aim to suit their bank.

Next, the executive trained the rest of the organization to understand Dr. Deming's principles. Now they are looking at each process in turn to learn its current level of quality and determine how to improve.

I know that this is only an example. An example teaches nothing without theory. However, here I learned something. I now have a theory for transformation.

First, it is from the top down. At each level in the organization there has to be an understanding of the principles of transformation. In addition to the understanding there has to be a conviction that this is

the right path for the firm. If enough executives believe in the process, a critical mass exists. Once we attain a critical mass, the process can go ahead.

The system of Profound Knowledge clearly shows the need for an aim. Once we determine the aim, we study each process. With knowledge of the process and its role in achieving the aim, we can make improvements.

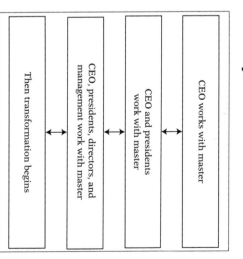

CEO works with master

CEO and presidents work with master

CEO, presidents, directors, and management work with master

Then transformation begins

7

The Seven Deadly Diseases

The Seven Deadly Diseases

The system of Profound Knowledge serves as a basis for change. The 14 Obligations are a method that managers can use to carry out this change. Blocking the transformation are the Seven Diseases and a myriad of obstacles.

We must fight the diseases directly to overcome them. They will kill off a company if not cured. We must understand the diseases (diagnose them) and then treat them through management action. Obstacles, damaging but not deadly, need similar management attention.

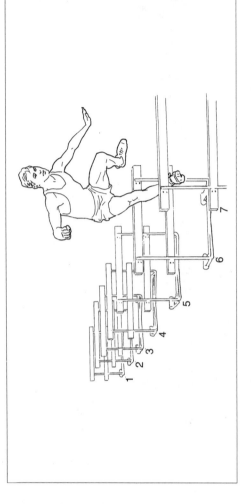

1. Lack of constancy of purpose
2. Emphasis on short-term profits
3. Evaluation of performance, merit rating, or annual review
4. Mobility of management, job hopping
5. Management by use only of visible figures, with little or no consideration of figures that are unknown or unknowable
6. Excessive medical costs
7. Excessive legal costs

Deadly Disease 1—Lack of Constancy of Purpose

Dr. Deming, with slow deliberation, explains that it is management's job to set future direction. Everyone needs to understand that vision. Workers need to know, suppliers need to know, even customers need to know. When there is no direction, then there is disease in the organization, then organizational direction is not like a cold or flu, it is not benign. Lack of a consistent organizational direction is deadly, it will send a company "down the tubes. . . ."

My friend, the owner of a trucking company, worked with a master. When they first met, the master asked my friend and his senior officers, What are you in business for? My friend asked his comptroller to explain it. The comptroller thought that they were in business to make as much profit as possible.

My friend then turned to the vice president of marketing and asked her to explain it. She said that they were in business to get the highest sales possible. Turning to the vice president of operations he asked him to explain the company. His view was that the purpose of their business was to deliver goods on time.

What does management care about this month?

What is our priority?

Where are we going?

None of these views matched my friend's ideas. He was in business to grow over the years and extend his share of market. With conflicting concepts, the top management of this firm was going in many directions at once. This is a good way for a business to go bankrupt.

This truly describes my company. Every five years we invent a new strategic vision that undoes past progress.

Fifteen years ago we were rich. Instead of reinvesting in our core business we started to diversify. Five years later, after getting into diverse businesses we did not make a profit. We hardly understood the new diversified businesses. We discovered we had bought other people's problems. As

another five years passed we were cost cutting in our vain attempt to turn our new acquisitions into profitable business units. Now we are trying to sell off our diversified businesses. In that way, we can raise money, buy back our stock, and position ourselves to avoid a takeover. What are we, managers, or just some big children tampering with the lives of our workers and our investors?

It never ends. Each of these shifts creates havoc on the front lines. The people on Wall Street have no idea of the real dollars lost through a lack of constancy of purpose. Yet Wall Street has little respect for or understanding of constancy of purpose. As nearsighted as we in management are, Wall Street is blind.

Deadly Disease 1—How to Develop Constancy of Purpose

Two basic problems face managers: problems of today and problems of tomorrow. Today's problems are the day-to-day issues of sales, production, budget, safety, etc. These are the daily requirements of current operations, the efforts to maintain our present business. We need to pay attention to these problems to stay in business.

Too many managers do not take any time to think about the future. Failure to take time to work on the problems of tomorrow exacts a penalty. The problems of today are for a large measure matters for which we did not provide in the past. That is, the problems of today are yesterday's problems of tomorrow that we did not work on.

A major failing of the Western style of management is the lack of planning. Some firms make grandiose five-year strategic plans, well documented but finally filed. The following year they repeat this farce.

Most such plans are financial or marketing wish lists. They fail to specify the necessary implementation method.

There are other problems of tomorrow, such as the development of new services that make life better for people, new methods of production, and new levels of service to customers.

Problems of Today
- Production levels
- Budget, sales, profits
- Employment, safety
- Service
- Public relations

Problems of Tomorrow
- New service and new product that may help people live better
- New materials required
- New methods of production
- New levels of performance in the hands of users

Managers must overcome the problems of both today and tomorrow. A manager cannot do it alone. By definition, a manager works through his or her people. His or her people need a direction, an aim. This requires managers to think through their purpose. Some companies will call this a mission statement, or a strategic plan. This must be articulated so others can understand and comprehend its meaning.

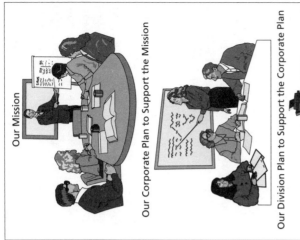

Our Mission

Our Corporate Plan to Support the Mission

Our Division Plan to Support the Corporate Plan

Our Department Plan to Support the Division Plan

Deadly Disease 2—Emphasis on Short-Term Profits

How do managers make profits these days? Mr. Robert Reich stated that there are many ways to make a profit. However, he continued, that is not the answer to our problems. A disease of what he calls 'paper entrepreneurialism' plagues us. Heavy pressure comes from Wall Street for short-term, quarter-by-quarter gains. These gains ignore variation, and each quarter they must go up. So managers rely on creative accounting, mergers, acquisitions, tax schemes, foreign currency swaps, and all sorts of finagling to boost the short-term profit. This disease, unchecked, will ruin our economy.

Dr. Deming feels that business schools teach exactly the wrong topics. "And they are doing very well," he says.

In my company the quarterly profit-and-loss statement drives us. No one gives a hoot about long-term profits. Toward the end of quarter we will take all kinds of action to make our numbers, never mind the future.

USA Business School

Registration

102 Paper Entrepreneurialism
103 Creative Accounting
104 Tax Dodging
105 Golden Parachutes
106 Leveraged Buy-out
107 Junk Bonds

I know we once loaded a customer up with products he couldn't really use but we showed a good end of year. We lost that customer, but no one cared, we made our bonus for that year.

Courses Not Taught

- System of Profound Knowledge
- Systems Thinking in the Workplace
- Understanding Variation
- Theory of Knowledge
- Theory of Psychology

Worldwide Steel Recession

Dr. Deming tells a gripping story of differences between America and Japan. In America, when the steel recession hit, top management recognized that they had a problem. They defined their problem as "How can we still pay a dividend when business is bad?" Their solution: cut costs. They laid off thousands, most of whom left the steel industry never to return.

In Japan, they saw the recession as a cyclical pattern. They understood variation. They asked themselves a very different question: "How can we prepare to expand our market share when the recession is over?" So they:

- **Cut back on take-home pay by dropping all bonuses. (Even Japanese line workers can have up to half their take-home pay as bonuses.)**
- **Sent engineers around the world to study customer future needs.**
- **Built a continuous-process furnace to off-load iron ore and to on-load finished steel with one giant conveyor belt.**

When the recession was over, the Japanese captured the market.

Worldwide Steel Recession

During a cyclical downturn the Japanese built a new mill. When business improved they captured the market. During the same downturn, American steel industry downsized and were ill prepared for the recovery.

In Baltimore, we had thousands of layoffs from Bethlehem Steel. When we lost these basic manufacturing jobs, the local economy suffered. We are still suffering. For each manufacturing job lost, we lose other jobs in retail, banking, government. Now I understand the reason for this. The American emphasis on short-term profits is killing us. It definitely is a disease. It would take courage for an American company to take a long-term approach and invest in the future. Now that I understand what the Japanese did, I see that we need a long-term approach.

A single company cannot do it alone. American investors will abandon them when profits go down. Isn't that what our business schools teach? Why should we invest in a company when profits are going down? In Japan, it is during a recession when profits are lowest that they invest in a continuous-process steel mill.

What is the implication of this story, what is the theory? Invest when profits go down? No, that cannot be the answer. Let me think. Dr. Deming is saying that we should apply Profound Knowledge.

First, appreciate that the steel industry is part of a system. For steel the system is a complex worldwide network containing diverse elements of people, machines, materials, methods, and environment. Management's job is to analyze the system. They must keep an eye on problems of today as well as those of tomorrow. Sure it's difficult, but that's our job.

We, as managers, need knowledge of many items. Among these are customer's current and future needs, engineering advances, and future opportunities for new business. We need knowledge of variation so we recognize a cyclical pattern when it occurs. If we treat each fluctuation up or down as a special cause and adjust our system, we call it tampering.

To stay in business, we need to adopt an entirely new philosophy of business. That's what this four-day lecture series is all about.

Deadly Disease 3—Evaluation of Performance, Merit Rating, or Annual Review

About forty years ago, North America became enamored with annual performance ratings. We thought such a procedure would elevate performance. In theory an annual review sounds helpful. It looks as though it makes sense. Every six or twelve months, supervisors rate subordinates on predetermined criteria. Psychologists mold the criteria, and some companies conduct training sessions for managers on how to determine ratings. In theory, the subordinate receives ratings and uses this feedback to improve.

The theory is to make employees better. Dr. Deming's voice deepens, his volume increases, his voice booms to the audience, "It does exactly the opposite." He walks to the overhead projector and writes while he speaks. "Let x equal the performance of the individual. Let y equal the performance of the system. Let xy represent the interaction of individual and system. Then x plus y plus xy equals the performance on which the annual rating depends.

"Here is the catch: x is unknown, and y is unknown. He who can solve a single equation with two unknowns can rate people. **It can't be done.**

"In practice, annual ratings are a disease, annihilating long-term planning, demolishing teamwork, nourishing rivalry and politics, leaving people bitter, crushed, bruised, battered, desolate, despondent, unfit for work for weeks after receipt of rating, unable to comprehend why they are inferior . . . sending companies down the tubes . . ."

I despise appraisals. I detest judging others or having them judge me. It strikes one as so unfair and arbitrary. Shouldn't a manager be a coach not a judge? I remember one of my first jobs. I only got a satisfactory rating. It haunted me for two years: hurt my confidence and slowed my pace. I lost respect for the supervisor and bailed out of the department.

In my company we do all our ratings in two months. The entire organization experiences trauma. Like the Titanic hitting the iceberg, a shudder runs through the ship. However, the damage is under the waterline, unseen until water floods the engine room. Dr. Deming suggests ratings are not just damaging but deadly.

We spend hours and hours for performance reviews, either in preparation or in meetings. We have endless discussions

Dr. Deming uses the notation X + [XY] where we normally use X + Y + XY. The authors followed Dr. Deming's notation system in the equation he made famous.

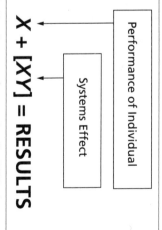

Performance of Individual

Systems Effect

X + [XY] = RESULTS

about how we should handle people. How will they react, how upset will they get? The employee usually hides the hurt and bitterness. Most display no emotion. However, internally, the psychological damage is unknown and unknowable. Sometimes, they drown the hurt and pain in alcohol or drugs. How do people explain to their families a low rating at work?

Deadly Disease 3—Evaluation of Performance, Merit Rating, or Annual Review (Continued)

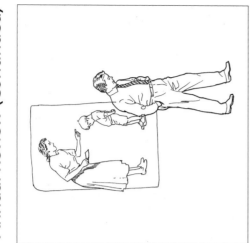

We treat adults like children with report cards, except that we don't require a parent's signature. While we are on report cards, let's get rid of these. The damage done to children by rating is horrendous. Many children stop learning. When will we understand variation? Children learn at different speeds. Grades will not improve this process.

Some psychologists argue that ratings point out our faults for correction. How does a person correct a low rating for cooperation? How can a personality trait change through a scoring process? The ratings are a poor substitute for leadership. Most people are part of a system. If the system does not operate under a theory of cooperation, then people will get low ratings in cooperation.

These psychologists do not understand variation. A person whose output is stable reacts to a rating by tampering, making the output worse.

Giving a rating is a destructive substitute for dealing with real issues of teamwork and cooperation. (I'm beginning to sound like Dr. Deming.)

Deadly Disease 3—Alternatives to Evaluations

Dr. Deming asks the audience: "Name a dozen people who have achieved success at an early age. Name them, who are they?" The audience begins to call out names, but in the end we have very few.

Dr. Deming exhorts us: "We'd go mighty hungry before going to lunch, if we had to name a dozen people who achieved success at an early age." (The audience does not laugh, but gets reflective; it's getting close to lunch time.)

"Are we too hasty in North America? Our aim should not be to become number one, rather it should be to improve all the time . . ." This takes leadership. A manager who relies on an annual rating will not prosper. Replace the annual performance review with leadership. A leader's job is then to be more careful in selecting people in the first place. Once you hire workers, it is your job to educate and train them so they know their jobs. Hold long interviews with them, three or four hours, to understand their views and the ways they desire to contribute. Use figures on performance not to rank people, but to discover who, if any, falls outside the system. Those outside the system need special attention or a transfer to another job.

Alexander the Great	age 22
Newton	age 22
Mozart	died at 33

Only a few have achieved success at an early age.

Deadly Disease 4—Mobility of Management

"In Japan, I met a man who worked for a meat packing company. For seven years he delivered meat. At 4:00 each morning he delivered to stores, hotels, and restaurants. He knew the disappointment of a customer who could not get the cut of meat he wanted. He knew the problems when a truck broke down. He understood the business. . . . After seven years, he was ready for management. Managers in Japan do not jump from company to company or from industry to industry. They have no mobility of management.

"Job hopping from company to company creates prima donnas for quick results. It annihilates teamwork, and teamwork is vital for continued existence."

During a social hour at a Silicon Valley chip fabricator I met a dozen or so American managers. To make small talk I asked each how long they had been with the company. Some said three years; others, five years; one, eight years. Their Japanese representative answered my question "fifteen years." He had more corporate history than anyone in the room. Isn't that interesting? We, Americans, are highly mobile and proud of it.

Headhunters argue that new people bring in new knowledge, new methods, new blood. Isn't it easier to get that information through competitive analysis, engineering, hands-on research rather than through mobility of management?

I climbed to my executive position through job hopping. I never wanted to stay too long in the same job, because others viewed this as topping out. If I go too long without a promotion, I job hop. At least it looks like a promotion. Also, it's dangerous to stay too long. The number games catch up. We talk of the "white knight syndrome." The "white knight" goes into a badly run area. He cleans it up and gets out fast. That's the way to fame and fortune. After you turn it around, bail out fast before the numbers catch up.

White Knight Syndrome
- Find an area that is a mess
- Go in as a saviour
- Make lots of changes—churn things up (tampering)
- Show results (short-term gains)
- Get rewards
- Leave before long-term problems appear

Deadly Disease 5—Running a Company on Visible Figures Alone

Dr. Deming says, "One cannot be successful on visible figures alone. Of course, visible figures are important:

To meet payroll
To pay suppliers
To pay taxes
To calculate depreciation
To fund contingencies.

"He who would run his company on visible figures alone will in time have neither company nor figures."

For my entire business career, I have been learning to manage by numbers. Now Dr. Deming says that management with visible figures only is a disease. Through business school we learned to analyze numbers. Even today we wouldn't dare go into a meeting without tons of numbers. In our companies we live and die by numbers. However, Dr. Deming is suggesting a different approach to numbers. He is making a distinction between visible and invisible numbers. Furthermore, he is suggesting that the invisible numbers are more important than the visible. He quotes Dr. Lloyd Nelson, "The most important figures needed for management of any organization are unknown and unknowable."

Credit Department

His example of the credit department is relevant. Dr. Deming explains that a credit department, doing its best, had succeeded in ridding the company of customers who did not pay promptly. The visible figures on promptness of payment showed a remarkable improvement. Only too late did the company learn that the accounting department had driven off some of the company's best customers.

From this lecture it occurs to me that most of the financial figures are really not good measurement tools. We are measuring short-term results. Financial figures don't help operations. Dr. Deming says the thermometer on the wall just tells the temperature of the room. It changes nothing. That's what our financial systems do.

Financial numbers tell about what happened last week, last month, or last quarter. They are historic data, about the past. Without an appreciation for a system and knowledge about variation we assume that historic data are a predictor of the future. I now understand about control charts. It is the calculation of control limits that gives us belief about the future. Many of the actions we take based upon historic data result in tampering.

When using visible figures only, the credit department drives out good customers.

Dr. Deming is saying that this perspective of examining only visible financial data is more than a problem, or a hindrance, or a weakness. He is saying it is a disease, a disease we must cure to survive. But what is the solution, what numbers can I use that are not visible? If they are not visible, then how can I use them? How can I use numbers that I cannot see?

Running a Company on Visible Figures Alone (Continued)

Dr. Deming's voice rises, he challenges us: "Where are the accounting people? Where are the financial people? Who has numbers on the multiplying effect of a happy customer? Who has numbers on the opposite effect from an unhappy customer? Where are numbers on improvement of quality and productivity from teamwork between engineers, production, sales, and marketing departments? Who has numbers for these items? Does anyone care about profits?" The audience is silent.

This is hitting close to home. We had a program to study costs associated with making bad items. The expert we called in told us that the solution was to measure four basic costs associated with poor quality.

He had us measuring how much we were spending on appraisal. Appraisal cost is the cost of checking and finding bad items in output. He also had us keep track of what he called "failure cost." This consists of two different costs depending on the location of detection. When detected at the point of production we call it "internal failure." When detected after the point of production we call it "external failure," detected downstream. Finally, he had us

measuring the costs associated with avoiding problems in the first place, the "prevention cost." We got reports on these costs and their sum, called "total cost." The idea was to reduce the total cost. What a mistake that turned out to be.

For one department the total cost was about $105,000 per year. They dealt directly with the customer. The whole department's operating cost was only $265,000. When we examined the cost components they broke down as follows:

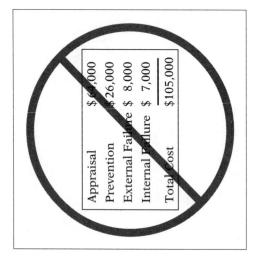

Appraisal	$ 64,000
Prevention	$ 26,000
External Failure	$ 8,000
Internal Failure	$ 7,000
Total Cost	$105,000

We thought that by reducing some prevention and appraisal costs we could make great savings. Even accounting for the slight increase in external failure costs, we expected to save a net of $45,000. This appealed to us. We made the changes and started to see the savings. The consultant was right.

For three months we felt good. Then came the blow. We lost an account worth $2,500,000 per year. The account noticed the degradation of our service. They told us that they could get better service elsewhere. We did not consider the unmeasurable costs, the unknown and unknowable costs that Dr. Lloyd Nelson talks about. When you look around carefully, you will see many such cost factors. What about the cost of employee morale? When processes run smoothly, employees are usually content with their jobs. When they have to adjust for a growing number of mistakes, they become more and more unhappy. We know that this impacts the output but cannot put a metric on this cost. Even the loss function described by Dr. Taguchi cannot include all of the unknown and unknowable costs.

Take Time to Understand the Figures

"If you can improve sales, productivity of quality by 5 percent without a rational plan, then why didn't you do it already? . . .

"If you are in a state of statistical control, the action you take on the appearance of a defect will cause more trouble. We need to improve the process by reduction of variation. Bill Scherkenbach stated one gets powerful leverage by going upstream in the study of the process."

As managers we learn that numbers are factual, flawless, and final. Now we are hearing that we must study the variation in numbers. What does this mean? When we study numbers, we are looking at differences between last month and this month, last quarter and this quarter, last year and this year. We also look at differences between Joe and John, Sue and Carol. Dr. Deming is suggesting that we don't really take the time and energy to understand the meaning of the figures we deal with. We don't have the knowledge to see variation, and then discover sources of variation. He seems to suggest that only through knowledge of the sources of variation can we truly make improvements. Change made without this knowledge is just tampering.

I am reading Scott Peck's book, The Road Less Traveled. In this book he describes himself as unable to make simple home repairs until he was 35 years old. He had always felt incompetent in this area. One day, his neighbor was repairing a lawn mower. Peck told his neighbor that he was unable to make such repairs. The handyman from next door explained: "Sure you can, if you only take the time." Peck pondered this theory.

Soon came the test of the theory. The emergency brake in a patient's car stuck. He crawled under the dash.

With his old self image he would have taken a cursory look and thrown up his hands in helplessness. Instead, he took the time to examine the wires, hoses, and cables. Slowly and thoughtfully he could trace the brake release, and find the stuck lever. The touch of a single finger released the brake. Peck confirmed his theory. By taking time one can do things that in the past seemed impossible.

We need to take time to trace and understand the sources of variation in our data. There is no instant pudding. To see the less-visible numbers we must take

time. To understand the invisible numbers we must take time into account.

I have heard American managers complain in their dealings with Japanese firms, that the Japanese take too long to decide what to do. (Yet once the Japanese make a decision, then they move ahead with higher sales and better products.) We in America are quick to implement a plan and content to work out the details by making adjustments in the field. As Tom Peters said, "Ready, Fire, Aim."

Although we save time in planning, we pay a much higher price through lower customer satisfaction. Now I understand the expression: "Why is there never time to do it right the first time, but always time to do it over?"

Study the Process, Not the Results Alone

Dr. Deming is suggesting that our companies are a series of components all strung together to form a system. The way they interact to achieve the aim of the system is the process.

We recognize that the most important numbers are unknown and unknowable. Worker behavior reacting to our leadership can have far-reaching effects. Yet we cannot measure these.

We just study visible figures, usually results. We manage by results. We have often heard, "Just show me the bottom line, I don't care how you got there."

Managers learn to examine results, outcomes. This is wrong. The manager's concern should be with processes. A good, fail-safe process delivers only good results. The concentration of a manager should be to make his processes better and better. To do so, he needs information about the performance of the process—the "Voice of the Process," as Mr. Scherkenbach calls it.[1]

Because of the complexity of the business, the processes interact with one another. Mr. Scherkenbach says there is powerful leverage in going upstream. What he is saying is that the manager should identify the initial process and get that to function properly. If the initial process is bad, the rest of the processes are poor or costly or both.

He is suggesting that we measure variation all along the process. This will be more effective the closer to the start of the process we can get. The process beginning, whether raw material or information, is a good start.

As managers, we can't do this all ourselves. We must give our people the knowledge and ability to study their own processes. In this way, they can better understand the sources of variation. Also, we can communicate with them in a common language to learn more about our systems.

There are prizes and awards designed to inspire companies to develop quality. They are results or outcome oriented. They pay lip service to process improvement but require results on which to make the awards. No wonder that some winners end up worse after winning the prize than they were before they followed the siren song to publicity.

Of course, it is nice to be recognized; but it should be for the right reasons.

[1] Scherkenbach, *op. cit.*, *Demings Road to Continual Improvement*, p. 11.

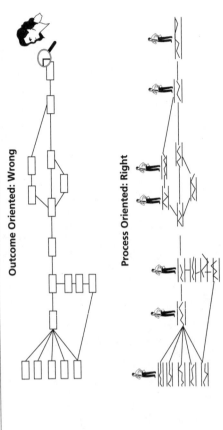

There is powerful leverage by going upstream

Outcome Oriented: Wrong

Process Oriented: Right

Deadly Disease 6—Excessive Medical Costs

"My friend, William E. Hoglund, manager of the Pontiac Motor Division, put it to me one day, 'Blue Cross is our second largest supplier. The cost of medical care is $400 per car.' Six months later he told me that Blue Cross had overtaken steel. That is not all. Additional medical costs are embedded in the steel that goes into an automobile."

Again Dr. Deming is showing why quality involves relationships between elements of a system. Just think, to improve competitive pricing of autos we must lower medical bills? In my company too, medical insurance is high. Before this moment I never thought that I must, and can, do something about it.

I've heard that the government has invented a method called Diagnostically Related Groups (DRGs). We talked about it in last night's study team. Apparently what was to be an improvement may have improved one aspect of the system, but made overall patient care worse.

The government set the standards. These are similar to the piece rate standards that Dr. Deming criticizes in Obligation 11. If the government says a particular procedure should require, on average, three days of hospitalization, then hospital administrators push doctors to release patients in three days or less. With little understanding of variation, hospitals are cutting back on patient care. In practice, the application of DRG standards suggests that most patients have the same needs, a questionable approach.

In the lecture Dr. Deming describes an entirely different approach to patient care. This approach incorporates variation. The aim of a

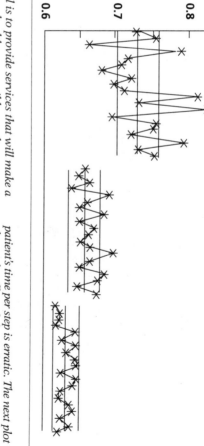

Time to Take a Step

hospital is to provide services that will make a patient as healthy as possible—and no more.

At a hospital in Japan a patient, after surgery, required physical therapy. He had to learn to walk again. To track progress, the staff measured the length of time it took the patient to take a step. They defined a step as the point when the patient's foot left the ground to the point when the same foot returned to the ground. They asked the patient to take 50 steps. Drs. Sugiyama and Hirokawa counted only the middle 10 successive steps (the 21st to 30th steps) to avoid "end" effects.

They recorded, on a control chart, the average time. They made twenty observations before physical therapy; twenty observations after ten days of treatment and twenty observations after three weeks of treatment. The control chart documents three distinct phases. First, before lessons,

patient's time per step is erratic. The next plot shows the effect of physical therapy. The patient requires less time per step but the process is still out of control. In the third stage, physical therapy has reached the end of its usefulness for this patient. A plot of the average time per step shows the walking process in control—progress has stabilized. Further therapy will not help the patient.

The system includes patient, physical therapist, equipment, and therapeutic approach. The stable control chart predicts that further treatment using this system will do no further good. Hospital administrators can conclude that physical therapy should end. This hospital, with these physical therapists and this patient, have done their best. Release this patient, spend no more money here.

Control charts offer a much better approach to hospital reform than do DRG standards.

Deadly Disease 7—Excessive Legal Costs

Dr. Deming tells the story of a Japanese executive who had a plaque on the wall saying one million parts shipped without a single defect. The next year a new plaque arrived—two million parts shipped without a single defect. Each year a new plaque would arrive. The supplier had so much pride in what he did, and the plaques kept arriving that he would never think of sending a defect. (Laughter)

Do they need a contract? The supplier's pride is on the line. He will do anything to keep the relationship going. In America we would have a contract and that would set up punishments for defective parts. But what good is a contract? It is much easier to break a contract than a relationship based upon pride. If you want to break a contract, just hire a lawyer. (Audience laughs, then applauds.)

A member of my last night's study team told a story of his bakery's twenty-year relationship with a fast food chain. Years ago the chain's founder called the baker and after they built a relationship, on a handshake they went into business together. The baker built factories for exclusive use by

the fast food chain. The fast food chain gave extensive territories to the baker. Over the years, the baker's sons went into the business, they grew and expanded and prospered. No contract, no lawyers, just trust between supplier and customer.

Dr. Deming suggests that the interested reader refer to Professor John O. Whitney's new book, The Trust Factor: Liberating Profits and Restoring Corporate Vitality, published by McGraw-Hill in 1993.

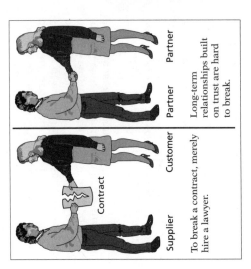

Supplier	Customer	Partner	Partner
To break a contract, merely hire a lawyer.	Contract	Long-term relationships built on trust are hard to break.	

The Seven Deadly Diseases

8

Obstacles

Obstacles to Getting the Job Done

We came to Dr. Deming's four-day seminar as skeptics. To be sure, before we arrived we had seen, read, and heard a lot about Dr. Deming and a whole jargon related to quality. We had heard terms such as:

- *Statistical Process Control (SPC),*
- *Quality Control Circles (QCC), and*
- *Quality Function Deployment (QFD).*

We had also heard of so-called "Total Quality Management (TQM)." This implies that quality is a method. Now I know that quality is actually an outcome and that the term "TQM" is misleading.

Our general view was that Japan was successful because of their culture, and that our workers, unions, and politicians caused our problems.

Some of us came to this lecture under duress. The thought of sitting in one room for four days is abhorrent for tough, action-oriented men and women like us. However, now we see the wisdom of Dr. Deming's approach. It takes more than four days to mull over past practices and to rethink our business.

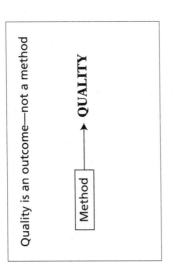

Quality is an outcome—not a method

Method ⟶ **QUALITY**

In Day One and Two, Dr. Deming got our attention. Then, recognizing that we want to change, he told us of the deadly diseases and obstacles. He didn't make it easy. Yet his prescription makes a good deal of sense. Common sense. Too bad that "common sense is not so common," as my friend, Commander Mike Romero, USN, used to say.

Obstacle—Hope for Instant Pudding

Dr. Deming gets our attention with a story: "I received a call. Come, spend a day with us, and do for us what you did for Japan; we too wish to be saved.

"I'd charge $50,000 if all they want is a day's help . . . that's because I would charge entertainer's prices." (Laughter)

In this next section we hear a discussion of obstacles we face in pursuit of better quality. We and our companies are actively pursuing strategies that really are obstacles to our success. Although some of us are aggressively trying to improve quality, many of our methods are the wrong approach.

Dr. Deming continues: "Dr. Lloyd S. Nelson sent me a copy of a letter he received which says:

"The president of my company has appointed me to the same position that you hold in your company. He has given me full authority to proceed, and he wishes me to carry on my new job without bothering him. What ought I to do? How do I go about my new job?'"

Dr. Deming adds, "It would be difficult to convey in a few lines so much misunderstanding."

Obviously, the writer's president looks upon quality as a method similar to accounting. Put someone in charge and it will happen. Nothing could be further from the truth. This explains the many failures of companies, which with best intentions, tried to "install" quality. Clearly, the writer's top management does not understand that quality is an outcome of their actions. It is also apparent that the writer knows less than his management, or he would not have accepted his task.

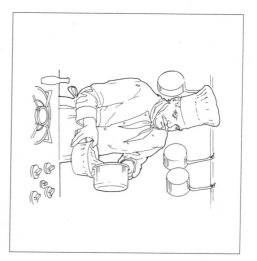

Obstacle—Hope for Instant Pudding (Continued)

It is good that I delayed appointing a VP of Quality until after this seminar. I wanted someone who would take responsibility for TQM, and just give me a report every month. (Or better yet, every three months.) I hoped that such a VP of Quality could solve my quality problems in about two years. Then I could eliminate the position. Now I understand that this would have been a disastrous move.

I heard of a prestigious American management consulting firm who promised a Canadian company instant results. The American management consultants promised to turn the Canadians from 8 percent return on investment to 14 percent return on investment in 90 days. Their method: fire 20 percent of the work force. Now I understand that in the short run, to make a quarterly P&L look good, cost cutting might create the impression of improvement. However, what happens to the work of the people we cut? In spite of the consultant's measurement, they were making a contribution.

As Mr. Latzko explained to me yesterday, it is a matter of understanding Queuing Theory. A draft of his paper

Cutting to the bone.

showed that as labor efficiency reaches 100 percent, the backlog becomes infinite. The service levels decline and the company goes out of business. What was the name of the bank in Long Island that experienced the same problem?

Living with the results after the hack is gone.

Are we sending our company down the tubes, just to look good in a particular quarter? Dr. Deming's advice comes to mind: "Don't export American management practices to friendly nations."

Obstacle—The Supposition that Solving Problems, Automation, Gadgets, and New Machinery will Transform Industry

Dr. Deming continues: "A plant at great expense installed automatic defect finding equipment. The equipment cut defects, but in doing so changed the nature of overall variation. Actual total variation increased.

"This company did not take the time and trouble to study and measure variation. If they had, they could have identified special causes of variation and ended those forever. They could continue to cut more and more causes of variation, improve their actual system and thus lower variation."

Dr. Deming refers us to Mr. William W. Scherkenbach's book, The Deming Route to Quality and Productivity. On page 30, Mr. Scherkenbach shows two charts similar to those pictured here. The bottom chart shows the control mechanism turned on. The output generates pieces covering the whole tolerance range. The top chart shows the control device turned off. The results are better. The distribution covers only a portion of the tolerance range.

If one understands the Loss Function developed by Dr. Taguchi, the top (Control Off) is better. The less variation and the closer the values are to the nominal value, the less the loss.

This explains Joe's reluctance to buy the adjusting gadget on his new tabletting machine. Joe is a plant manager for a large pharmaceutical company: In his plant he produces the bulk of the company's over-the-counter analgesic tablets. The production of these medicines consists of carefully compounding the ingredients that are then tabletted. The machine measures the powdered material and compresses it between two matched punches. This forms the tablet. The tablet weight is critical since it is proportional to dosage. A major product line in Joe's plant weighed 500 milligrams (mg). Government standards permitted a variation of ± 15 percent. While this gave a range of 425 to 575 mg, Joe had maintained a much better control over his product.

Joe's experience was similar to that of Mr. Scherkenbach. The corporate engineers insisted that Joe test the $150,000 "enhancement" to his machine. Joe did so. He had attended Dr. Deming's seminar and studied his work. He knew that this device followed Rule 2 of the funnel experiment. As a result he expected at least a 41 percent increase in variation (see page 152). As it happened, the equipment performance was worse than feared. The bottom chart shows a radical increase in the variation.

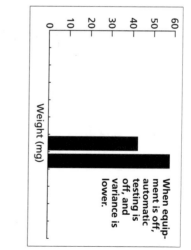

When equipment is off, automatic testing is on, and variance is lower.

When equipment is on, automatic testing is on, and variance is higher.

Weight (mg)

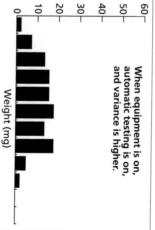

Weight (mg)

Effect of automatic testing equipment.

Obstacle—The Search for Examples—Examples without Theory Teach us Nothing

Central
Limit
Theorem

Ohio

Dr. Deming continues: "It is not unusual for a consultant to receive an inquiry for an example of success in a similar product line. One man inquired if these methods had ever been used in the manufacture of wheelchairs. Another inquired about compressors for air conditioners: Did I know of any application? My answer to such inquiries is that no number of examples of success or failure would indicate what success a company would have. Success depends on an understanding of the Theory of Profound Knowledge, an appreciation of the 14 Obligations and of the diseases and obstacles, and the efforts that he puts forth."

In a chat during the break, Dave Chambers, one of Dr. Deming's helpers, confirms Dr. Deming's experience. "I once received a call: We are interested in quality improvement. You were recommended. Our company is located in Ohio—have you ever done consulting with a company in Ohio? My reply: I do believe the Central Limit Theorem holds true in Ohio."

I do not expect my corporate attorney to have a degree in mechanical engineering. Nor do I expect my accountant to have this kind of background.

I read about this new concept called "benchmarking." A definition I read stated that benchmarking is finding the best in class. Once identified, focus on the processes that made these companies the best in their class. What could be more dangerous? To copy an example without understanding the theory is inviting disaster. Conditions are different among different companies. The customer base is different. One cannot copy processes blindly. What I need is a theory of management that will make my company successful. Studying other companies without theory is useless. I would not even know what questions to ask to get information.

Obstacle—The Search for Examples—Plant Tours Teach Nothing without Theory

Dr. Deming says, "Too often this is the story. Management of a company has a desire to improve quality and productivity. They know not how to go about it. They have not guidance from principles. Seeking enlightenment, they embark on excursions to other companies that are ostensibly doing well.

"They are received with open arms, and the exchange of ideas begins. They (visitors) learn what the host is doing, some of which may by accident be in accordance with the 14 Obligations."

"Devoid of guiding principles, they are both adrift. Neither company knows whether or why any procedure is right, nor whether or why another is wrong. The question is not whether a business is successful, but why? And why was it not more successful?"

I have wondered about the value of these plant tours, especially the way we do them. I have often seen people on tours of other plants. They come back with all sorts of ideas—one set of consultants called them "best business practices." Today's catchy term is "benchmarking." These big ideas usually fall short of expectations. Why is that?

Now I understand. When we copy examples, we miss the overall context. We ignore the Theory of Profound Knowledge (systems, variation, knowledge, and psychology).

We overlook the fact that the best business practice or benchmark comes from a different system. We overlook the fact that a different set of variables impacts their system than impacts ours. We overlook the fact that we have limited knowledge of their facility. The culture of the people from one plant to the next is different. When we make these visits we ask "What" and "How." We don't ask "Why" and "By what method?"

I have often seen a person doing a superb job in one location. When we transfer this person to another location, he fails. We find equipment functioning perfectly in location A, so we buy it for location B only to have the disappointment of failure. Success without a theory to explain the success does not contribute to knowledge.

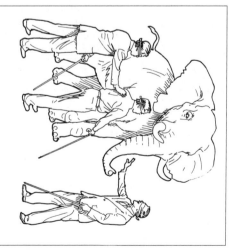

The Blind Men and the Elephant
One blind man feels the trunk and thinks it is a snake. Another feels the leg and thinks it is a tree. A third touches the body and thinks it is a wall.

Copying Japanese Quality Control Circles

Dr. Deming is urging us to start with a theory, a belief, a guess, a hunch, and then test it in real life, gather data. Compare these data with our theory. How do they compare? Do they support our theory? If yes, then we have learned something. If no, then we have also learned. This is the scientific method applied to the workplace. This is the method Edison used to invent the light bulb. He tested material after material until he found tungsten.

The owners of one successful company parked a 1935 Ford pickup truck in the basement garage. Without theory we might erroneously conclude that the company's success is due to the antique pickup truck parked in the garage. We would then have a best business practice (a benchmark) that we would duplicate in other plants. Hack consultants tell us, "Be assured of success, copy a best business practice."

To know why another company is successful, we would need to understand their system of customers and suppliers. We also would need to look at their process steps and the variation in those steps. We would need knowledge of their theories about business practices, and then we would need knowledge of their psychology.

Is this not like America's early experience with Quality Control Circles? Some Americans went over to Japan in the late 1960s. They went to see what made the Japanese so competitive. Japanese manufacturers showed them their methods including their latest methods, Quality Control Circles. Our observers assumed that all the American companies had to do was to copy Japanese Quality Control Circles. This would give us the Japanese success. Without Profound Knowledge of systems, variation, knowledge, and psychology, merely copying provides only short-lived improvements.

The reason that the so-called Total Quality Management (TQM) is not working here is that we are merely trying to copy what the Japanese do. The very name is a distraction. It implies that quality is a method. It is not a method, it is an outcome. The method is modern management based on the system of Profound Knowledge.

Managers misled by the words "Total Quality Management" think that one need only hire an expert in "Quality" and all troubles will disappear. They will be disappointed.

Obstacle—The Search for Examples—It Is a Hazard to Copy

Dr. Deming continues: "During a seminar I heard about the management of a company that makes furniture. They were doing well. They took it into their heads to expand their line into pianos. Why not make pianos?

"They bought a Steinway and took it apart. They measured each part. They made or bought parts according to the measurements. They put a piano together exactly like the Steinway, only to discover that they could only get thuds out of their product. They decided therefore not to expand from furniture to pianos.

"Thinking they at least could recoup their losses, they reassembled the Steinway intending to get their money back—only to discover that it too would now only make thuds." (Laughter)

Dr. Deming is saying that it takes Profound Knowledge for a company to operate successfully and to change from one field to another. They must have studied musical theory and instrument making. An American company that wanted to grow from making furniture to pianos would have to gain knowledge of musical theory.

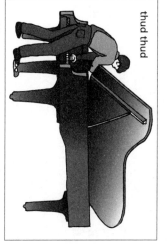

thud thud

Good furniture makers cannot make pianos without knowledge of music and harmonics.

They should start on a small scale. It might take an entire generation from father to son before realizing the new capability. Instead we want instant results we can see next year or even next quarter.

The Problem with Benchmarking

In November 1992, I took a trip to Japan. It surprised me to see that most of the companies I visited had passed from father to son. They take a long-term approach to their business, possibly because they know that their sons will go into their businesses. Robert Bly comments on this topic in his best-seller Iron John. *He talks of the loss a man feels when his son does not go into his business. Again, Dr. Deming's lecture is making me think about my entire life, not merely the workplace. (I'm going to pass these lecture notes along to my daughter.)*

Today many companies are talking about benchmarking. To me, benchmarking is a fancy name for copying. To select the "best in class" without understanding why it is best leads to disaster. Without understanding the theory needed to convert someone else's process to our use, we apply the process as the originator did. This can be completely wrong.

In 1953 Dr. Joseph Juran taught the Japanese his method of Managerial Breakthrough. Dr. Kaoru Ishikawa learned the theory of Managerial Breakthrough. He applied this to the Japanese conditions. The result was Quality Control Circles. If American observers had understood the theory, they would revert to Dr. Juran's method for this country.

The Japanese appear to take a more intelligent approach. They do not copy, but rather they learn why something works. Then they can make it better. Here again is an example of the application of the system of Profound Knowledge.

In my company we have suffered a number of losses due to copying without the knowledge of why something is working.

Obstacle—Obsolescence in Schools

Dr. Deming carries on: "Schools of business in America teach students that there is a profession of management, that they are ready to step into top jobs. This is a cruel hoax.

"Most students have had no experience in production or in sales. To work on the factory floor with pay equal to half what he hoped to get upon receipt of the MBA, is a horrible thought to an MBA, not the American way of life. As a result, he struggles on, without real factory experience, unaware of his limitations or unable to face the need to fill in the gap. The results are obvious."

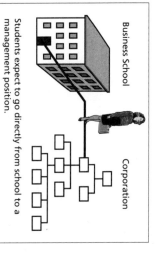

Business School

Corporation

Students expect to go directly from school to a management position.

I have seen this so often. Young graduates are intelligent, full of energy, and ready to work. They want and expect to start at a supervisory or management job, thinking that what they learned can readily apply to the real world. However, without the benefit of a system of Profound Knowledge, their preparation is incomplete. They know little of the system, variation, philosophy, or psychology. Yet they expect to be in management.

Hope exists. A little brochure on Fordham University's Deming Scholars MBA Program encourages me. It contains five cycles of learning that build upon the system of Profound Knowledge. (Maybe my daughter will apply.)

- *Cycle 1: Introduce the system of Profound Knowledge.*
- *Cycle 2: Deepen understanding of the system of Profound Knowledge.*
- *Cycle 3: Develop understanding of measurement.*
- *Cycle 4: Develop strategies for leadership of transformation through understanding of organizational learning and optimization of a system.*
- *Cycle 5: Deepen understanding of cultural formation and change and optimization of the enterprise.*

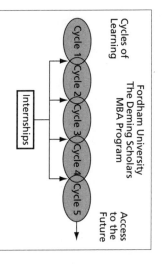

Cycles of Learning

Fordham University
The Deming Scholars
MBA Program

Cycle 1 Cycle 2 Cycle 3 Cycle 4 Cycle 5

Internships

Access to the Future

Obstacle—Poor Teaching of Statistical Methods in Industry

Dr. Deming states: "Awakening to the need for quality, and with no idea what quality means nor how to achieve it, American management has resorted to mass assemblies for crash courses in statistical methods, employing hacks for teachers, unable to discriminate between competence and ignorance. The result is that hundreds of people are learning what is wrong."

My friend has a company that makes ball bearings. He made every mistake Dr. Deming talks about. His customers demanded that he get into quality. He trained hundreds of workers in Statistical Process Control (SPC). Weeks later all SPC activity died off. He thought that the computations and data gathering was too difficult. To ease the process, he installed computers to do SPC on line. Within weeks the interest waned. No one in management had bothered to use the results of the computations. How could they use them? They had no training in SPC, much less managing for quality at SPC. For their third try at SPC, they were fortunate to get a master. He insisted that my friend and his management

staff learn about the system of Profound Knowledge and Dr. Deming's 14 Obligations. When they understood this aspect of their job, he trained them in SPC. He made them use this method before they asked any worker to use it. Quality comes from the action of the top management. Now I understand why training of operators in SPC is not enough. The improvement of quality is much more than creating a few control charts.

In these three days I have come to appreciate that numbers come mostly from the system, not from people. People are only part of the system. I have been quick to criticize, cajole, and browbeat individual workers, supervisors, and managers when numbers are not to my liking. I am good at it. Sometimes I threaten like a football coach talking to the bench: "When are you fellows in marketing going to get off your butts and pump up some numbers?" Everyone gets the message, i.e., Fear. I have often said, "I don't care how you do it, just make those numbers."

As the boss I watched, without understanding, our first attempts to install SPC. That's just what I wanted to do, install SPC and be done with it. Qualify for ISO 9000 and go on to other problems. I know better now. There is so much more to learn.

Obstacle—Use of Military Standard 105D and Other Tables of Acceptance

Dr. Deming continues: "Many thousands of dollars' worth of product changes hands hourly, lots subjected to acceptance or rejection, depending on tests of samples, drawn from the lots. Examples of such plans are Military Standard 105D, and Dodge-Romig AOQL (average outgoing quality limit) or Dodge-Romig LTPD (lot tolerance percentage defective). Such plans can only increase costs [for nondestructive testing]. If used for quality audit of final product as it goes out the door, these plans guarantee that some customers will get defective product. The day of such plans is finished. American industry cannot afford the losses that they cause."

A participant told the following story: An American computer manufacturer ordered parts from a Japanese supplier. The Americans had tried to make the parts but experienced a large percentage of noncon-forming items. In typical American fashion they specified a sampling plan (Department of Defense MIL-STD-105D) with an "Acceptable Quality Level" (AQL) of .04. If the supplier has a process average of 4 defective parts per 10,000 or better, the sampling plan assures him of a high chance of accepting the lot. The American manufacturer thought that their new Japanese supplier could not make 10,000 parts with only 4 defects and still make money on the deal. It is a purchasing manager's game called "squeeze the supplier."

The shipment arrived all in good order. Within the carton was a separate box, neatly wrapped with this note: "We Japanese have a hard time understanding North American Business Practices. The four defective parts per 10,000 have been included and are wrapped separately. Hope this pleases."

[The latest version of this Military Standard is MIL-STD 105E, Sampling Procedures and Tables for Inspection by Attributes. This standard is also called the ABC standard. ABC stands for American, British, and Canadian. It is the authors' opinion that the most recent version of these standards is not as good as the previous version.]

Gentlemen:
We Japanese have a hard time under-standing North American Business Practices. The four defective parts per 10,000 have been included and are wrapped separately. Hope this pleases.

10,000 Electronic Parts

4

9

The Funnel

Management and Tampering

The story of how Dr. Walter Shewhart became involved in a problem that led to the development of the control chart is told on page 98. We learned that his work at the Hawthorn Plant introduced two new ideas, random and assignable causes of variation. Today we call these common and special causes of variation. What makes these ideas so important?

The management action we take is entirely different when faced with common or with special causes of variation. For special causes of variation, managers must figure out what produced the unusual result. It probably requires corrective action. We may find that it was a unique situation, or it may be something that could happen again. As managers we examine what, if anything, we need to do to prevent the recurrence of the special cause of variation.

For common causes of variation, the management action is very different. The common causes are inherent in the process. We can predict that they will occur repeatedly. That is, they will recur unless we make a fundamental

change in the process. This means changing a process characteristic such as the equipment, material, method, environment, or factor related to the workers. We must change one or more of these key factors.

Confusion of the two conditions leads to tampering. That is, the management action ends in making matters worse. This was what seemed to happen at Hawthorn. Management considered every deviation from specification as a special cause of variation. Some probably were due to a special

cause. But more of these deviations were due to common causes. By treating every deviation as a special cause, management made things worse.

Dr. Shewhart gave us an operational definition of a special cause, the control chart. A point falling on or outside the control limits is a special cause of variation. These points merit management's immediate attention. Nonrandom points within the control limits are also an indication of a special cause. Random points falling within the control limits are common causes of variation.

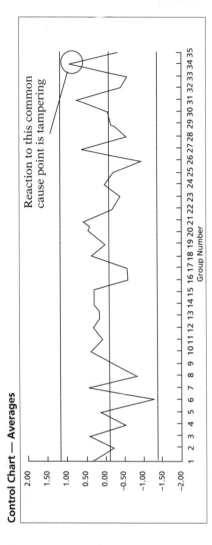

Control Chart — Averages

Reaction to this common cause point is tampering

Group Number

Dr. Shewhart's Experiment

In his book, *The Economic Control of Quality of Manufactured Product*, Dr. Shewhart describes his experimentation to find a model that would balance the two mistakes. These mistakes are

1. Calling an observation a special cause when it is a common cause of variation, or

2. Calling an observation a common cause when it is a special cause of variation.

In doing the experiment, Dr. Shewhart used a large salad bowl filled with metal-rimmed coat tags. On each coat tag he had written a number. The bowl and the coat tags represented his process. Dr. Shewhart drew 4,000 samples of the coat tags for each of three distributions. (The bowl and some coat tags survived. One can see them at the American Society for Quality Control in Milwaukee.)

For every one of four consecutive drawings he computed six statistics. He made these computations in the early 1920s when calculators and computers were unknown.

Dr. Shewhart concluded that the most economical balance between the

two errors occurred when he used a model of the mean plus or minus three standard deviations. This became the model of the Shewhart control chart named after its inventor.

We call the mean plus three standard deviations the "upper control limit" and call the mean minus three standard deviations the "lower control limit." We define points falling randomly within these two limits as common cause of variation. Reacting to a point from the common cause of variation as though it represented a special cause of variation causes tampering.

Tampering is an important subject to me and my business. I wonder how much tampering I do when I review our financial results and react to the message they seem to give. My friend in the logistics business was telling me that he uses control charts to run his business. I didn't realize the implication of his actions.

The numbers we use to run a business fluctuate normally. When the fluctuation is small, we pay no heed to it. When the fluctuation is large, we want to take action. We all have a different opinion of

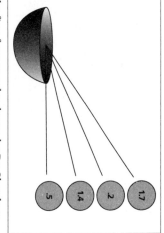

The first four samples drawn by Dr. Shewhart.

what is a large fluctuation. If we settle on a fluctuation that is really from the common cause system, we are tampering, making matters worse. In this context, a large fluctuation means a special cause of variation.

What about those fluctuations that are not special causes yet signal poor operating conditions? My friend said that since he uses control charts on his financial indicators, he has been far more successful in resolving problems. He now attacks the special causes of variation as something requiring a key change in the process. He has put management teams to solving these problems. The result is a totally improved operation. It is no longer a wonder to me that he likes the use of control charts.

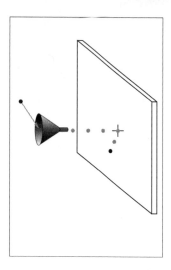

The Funnel Experiment

As we have just seen, the purpose of statistical thinking is to allow managers to act rationally. Special causes are examined at once, their cause determined, and corrective action taken. Common causes of variation present another problem. If the variation of the process is too large, the manager must work on making one or more basic changes in the elements of the process to affect improvement in the process.

The question arises: **What if we ignore these principles? What happens if we run our business with no clue as how to handle variation?** Generally, if a manager does not know whether a flaw or defect or adverse financial number is a special cause, he will act as though it were a special cause. He will feel that it is safer to take action than to be criticized for failing to act. What will be the result? Tampering is the outcome if a manager mistakes a common cause as a special cause of variation.

To illustrate several common forms of tampering, Dr. Deming uses an experiment employing a funnel. Dr. Lloyd Nelson suggested the original idea of the use of a funnel.

"We are going to conduct a simple experiment. We won't actually do the experiment here, but I will describe it to you and you will understand the implications.

"Imagine that we have a funnel, a stand to hold the funnel about a half meter above a table, and on the table we have a target. Imagine that we drop a marble down the funnel. The marble will roll down the funnel in a random fashion, regardless of how we might make the drop. The marble then falls from the bottom of the funnel and we mark the spot on the table with a pencil. Simple.

"We will follow certain rules for aiming the funnel over the target. These rules correspond to decision rules we make in running equipment, processes, and systems."

Rule 1—We Make No Adjustment to the Funnel

"The marble as it rolls around the funnel and finally out the end (much like a roulette wheel) is being acted upon by the random forces of friction, gravity, and harmonics. These forces produce a great many common (random) causes of variation, but the system is stable.

"If we keep the funnel in its holder and the target and table steady, the marble will fall in a random pattern around the target. It won't land in exactly the same spot because of the action by the random forces mentioned above.

"But after the first 50 drops we can readily and with some confidence predict the next 50 drops and the next and the next. We can't predict too far into the future, because our system may change."

Let me see, how can the system change? The bar that holds the funnel may become loose, which could produce a special cause of variation. We might observe a trend in our data (perhaps caused by a loose screw). We must investigate and find the source of the special cause of variation. If it turns out to be a loose screw on the holder, then tighten the screw.

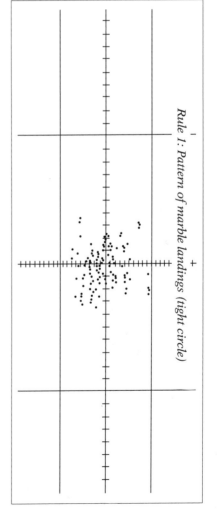

Rule 1: Pattern of marble landings (tight circle)

We could then add a method to prevent future occurrences, such as checking the screw every 200 drops. We might then change our prevention method to checking every 400 drops until we found how to prevent this special cause (loose screw) from occurring in the most economical way.

"In this example we make 50 drops of the marble. If we mark where each drop landed, we will get a diagram as shown above. The marble pattern is that of a circle clustered about the target. We can predict that addi-

tional throws of the marble will also land within the circle. Management's job is prediction. Our system is not perfect. The marble does not always hit the bull's eye."

We learned in the lesson of the red beads that the worker, who makes the drops, or who marks the target, or who built the table, cannot really do much to improve performance.

As managers we want to come closer to the target. One method managers use to hit the bull's eye more often, Rule 2, is described on the following page.

Rule 2—Adjust the Funnel from Its Last Position Vis-à-Vis Target

"How can we hit the bull's eye more often? In Rule 1, the funnel was kept in the same position every time. We made no adjustment for 'drift.' In Rule #2, we need to measure the direction and the distance that the marble landed away from the target. Then, we move the funnel from its present position in an equal and opposite direction.

"If the marble landed 15 cm to the North West (NW) we move the funnel 15 cm to the South East (SE). Now we drop the marble again and measure the point where it lands. (See top left figure.)

"This time the marble lands 22 cm to the North East (NE). The adjustment under Rule 2 is to move the funnel from where it last dropped the marble to position 22 cm away in the South West (SW) direction. (See the top right figure.)

"If we continue this exercise many times and record each time where the marble landed, we see that the pattern is again circular but the pattern covers a much larger area than it does with Rule 1. Theory tells us that the pattern will be 41% larger."

(Rule 2 doubles the variance. The standard deviation is the square root of the variance. The square root of 2 is approximately 1.41. Therefore, the dispersion is approximately 41% larger than it is in Rule 1.)

Rule 2 was the driving force in the examples cited on page 137. These examples were about equipment that measured

parts and self-adjusted in an equal but opposite direction from the measurement to the nominal value. In all such instances, the variation increased.

Another area where Rule 2 helps to destroy stable processes is in the insistence on the regular calibration of equipment. Far better is the policy of measuring the equipment and recording the results on a control chart. When the chart suggests the presence of a special

cause, then we might calibrate the equipment. Remember that equipment is part of a system of measurement. Other factors such as operator, environment, etc. affect the outcome. A change in any factor can require adjustment.

The Defence Logistics Agency insists on my calibrating and adjusting all my equipment on a regular schedule. They just don't know what they are doing with regard to calibration.

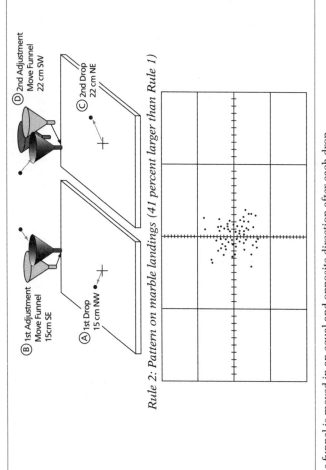

B 1st Adjustment Move Funnel 15cm SE

A 1st Drop 15 cm NW

D 2nd Adjustment Move Funnel 22 cm SW

C 2nd Drop 22 cm NE

Rule 2: Pattern on marble landings (41 percent larger than Rule 1)

The funnel is moved in an equal and opposite direction after each drop.

Rule 3—Bring back to Origin Before Adjustment

Rule 2 increased the variation—instead of improving the process, Rule 2 made it worse. There is something wrong with the model we chose. Let's examine our model more closely.

In Rule 1 we left the funnel alone. It sat in place. Because of our inaction, the marble could drift around the target. In Rule 2 we wanted to improve the result by taking the drift of the marble into consideration. The result was not encouraging; the pattern of Rule 2 was worse than Rule 1. On considering what could have happened, we find that there is one weak point in the way we formulated Rule 2. The funnel for Rule 2 moved from its last position to the next position. The funnel moved but the target did not move. Perhaps the answer is to bring the funnel back to its original position before adjusting. This method is Rule 3.

In Rule 3 the first drop is again 15 cm NW from the target. The funnel is situated at its original position. Therefore, the first move under Rule 3 is the same as Rule 2. We move the funnel 15 cm to the SE. (See upper left diagram.)

The next drop comes to rest 22 cm NE of the target. We now move the funnel in two steps. Step 1, move the funnel to its original position. Step 2, move the funnel from its original position 22 cm to the SW. (See upper right diagram.)

Recording the location of each marble, we see that a new, strange pattern emerges.

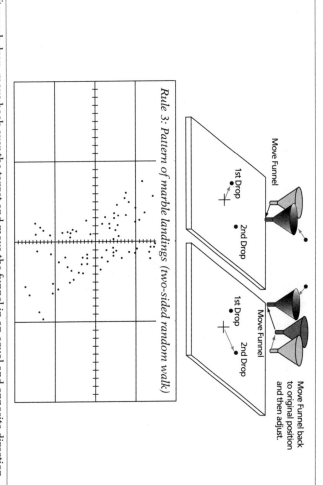

Rule 3: Pattern of marble landings (two-sided random walk)

After each drop, move back over the target and move the funnel in an equal and opposite direction.

The pattern is bow-tie shaped. It is ever increasing—as Dr. Deming says, "Off to the Milky Way."

Where does this type of management system operate? Unfortunately, it occurs in many places. One illustration is the adjustment of this month's budget based on last month's variance.

Dr. Deming gives other illustrations:

- Nuclear proliferation
- Barriers to trade
- Illicit drug intervention
- A gambler increases his bet to cover losses

Move Funnel

1st Drop   2nd Drop

Move Funnel

1st Drop   2nd Drop

Move Funnel back to original position and then adjust.

Rule 4—Aim at the Previous Point

It is obvious that **Rule 2 and Rule 3** did not get us closer to the target. **Indeed,** the opposite is true: We are worse off than we were when using Rule 1. On considering this phenomenon we conclude that moving the funnel to account for drift is not rewarding. Perhaps it is best to try and get the place where the marbles land to cluster as close as possible, even if this is not on the target.

To carry out this model, we use **Rule 4:** Place the funnel on top of where the previous marble landed. This means that if our marble landed 15 cm NW we move the funnel on top of the resting place of the first marble. (See left top diagram in illustration.)

The next drop of the marble lands 7 cm North West (NW) from the target. We place the funnel over this point. As we continue to make adjustments according to Rule 4, we notice that the pattern of where the marbles land first moves around the target. As we proceed, the pattern of the marbles starts to move in a single direction away from the target. As Dr. Deming says, the movement is "off to the Milky Way." Unlike Rule 3, Rule 4 goes only in one direction.

The most common form of this type of tampering exists in almost every industry, government, and academic institution. Many of these organizations "train" their new employees by having the incumbent employee explain the job to the newcomer. Then we wonder why people do things

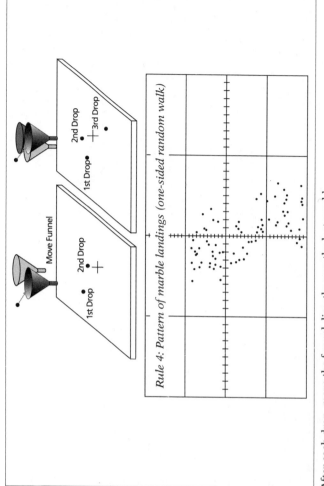

Rule 4: Pattern of marble landings (one-sided random walk)

After each drop, move the funnel directly over the last marble.

wrong. It was the way we trained them, worker training worker.

In another example, **Dr. Deming** tells the story of the man who followed **Rule 4** when he cut 100 "two-by-fours" each 64 inches long. Instead of using a ruler for each cut, he used the previously cut piece of lumber. If each cut was about ⅛ inch longer than the previous one, the graph shows how each piece of wood grew.

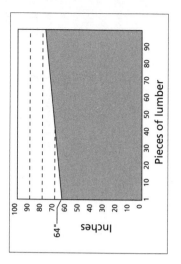

What Does It All Mean to Me

What Dr. Deming showed was very important to me. Until now, I had no idea that some actions that I am taking could result in outcomes exactly opposite to what I want.

Dr. Deming's books, Out of the Crisis, (pages 327–333) and The New Economics for Education, Government and Industry (Chapter 9), explain in more detail the four rules of the funnel.

In Rules 2 through 4 we acted as though every drop of the marble resulted in a special cause point. We reacted to every deviation from normal. We did not understand that the point where the marble landed is the result of a system that has variation. We considered each point to be absolute and a true value. From the system of Profound Knowledge, we know that there is no such thing as a true value. Change the method of measurement, and you change the result.

By acting as though each drop of the marble was a special cause, when in fact it was a series of common causes, we tampered. When I think about what this simulation means to my company, I become frightened. How often do we make management decisions based on

financial data, where all we see is the target and the last drop of the marble?

When I get back to the office, I must look into the use of arbitrary percentages to control our operations. Why can't we get financial and other operating data in the form of a control chart? Then we would know whether the observed results are from a special cause or come from a common cause system. We would know what type of action to take.

My friend Jim Dowhin runs a large warehousing operation. He uses control charts to run his business. He worked with one of Dr. Deming's disciples to learn how to do this. They published a paper about how he used the charts.[1]

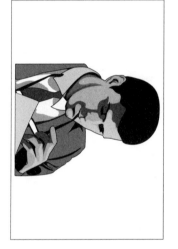

My company is going to use control charts. I have also learned that the most important numbers are unknown and unknowable. This means that I am going to be very cautious in the use of data. We have to make our decisions with all the knowledge and experience available to us in the company.

[1]See Latzko, W. J. and J. D. Dowhin, "Achieving Service Quality by Charting" in the Forty-Fifth Annual Quality Congress Proceedings, (Milwaukee, American Society for Quality Control, 1991). See also Latzko, W. J., "Control Charts in the Board Room" in the Forty-Third Annual Quality Congress Proceedings, (Toronto, American Society for Quality Control, 1989).

10 *Operational Definitions*

DAY FOUR   DAY THREE   DAY TWO   DAY ONE

Operational Definitions

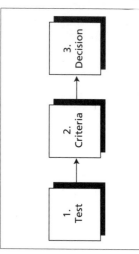

D r. Deming says, "In the opinion of many people in industry, there is nothing more important for the transaction of business than the use of operational definitions. It could also be said that nothing is more neglected."

An operational definition generally has three parts. These parts—test method, criterion (or criteria), and decision—are not inherently good or bad, they just represent a system for communicating and measuring. Remember that the Theory of Knowledge tells us there is no such thing as a true value. The result obtained depends on the method used for examining the item.

Without operational definitions we have no common language. The meaning in one person's mind is different from the meaning in another person's mind. To get agreement in people's minds we need operational definitions of any specification, standard operating procedure, instruction, measure, or regulation. Operational definitions allow everyone to come to the same conclusion. Their meaning is the same today as it is tomorrow.

1. A test is conducted that gives data on criteria.
2. Decide the criterion for judgment.
3. Based upon the test and criteria a decision is made:

   ☐ Yes Criteria met
   ☐ No   Criteria not met

We cannot deal with vague definitions. For example, "Moisture content of the paper must be between 4 and 5 percent." By what method do we decide the moisture content? One could use the oven drying method of ASTM Method D 644 or the Toluene distillation method TAPPI Standard T 484. Ainsley and Underhay reported that the latter method gives slightly higher readings than the former method.

When the National Bureau of Standards (now known as the National Institute of Standards and Technology, NIST) changed its method of measuring gauge blocks from mechanical instruments to laser units, all the dimensions underwent a small change. No matter how finely finished a gauge block appears, with enough magnification one can detect small hills and valleys on the surface. Mechanical tools measure the highest hill. Laser tools penetrate into the valleys. The results are minuscule differences. These differences are important in industries making ultrafine parts.

How Many People Are in the Room

Although we use operational definitions (test, criteria, and decision) these do not give us a true value. Operational definitions are only a system for communicating and measuring.

Dr. Deming asks the audience, "How many people are in the room?" He pauses for a moment and then repeats, "How many people are in the room?" We look around, apparently hundreds and hundreds, but some are standing, some are sitting, some are walking through the door going out, some are coming in. The audience looks around quizzically. "How many people are in the room?" His voice booms through the loudspeaker.

"Why are we asking? Is it for registering those who are attending, is it for ordering lunch, is it for arranging chairs, or is it for the fire marshal's inspection?

"For each purpose we would have unique criteria. For each criterion we would have a unique procedure for counting. And for each method of counting we would have a different number.

"The answer depends upon the purpose of the question. We need an operational definition.

Question: How many in the room
Purpose: For income generated
Method: Number paid in advance, plus the number paid at the door, plus the number to be billed

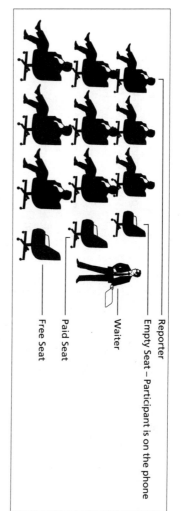

Reporter
Empty Seat – Participant is on the phone
Waiter
Paid Seat
Free Seat

Question: How many in the room
Purpose: For number of chairs
Method: Number registered, and the number of free registrations, plus 10 percent for walk-ins

Question: How many in the room
Purpose: For water glasses
Method: Number registered, plus the number of free registrations, plus 10 percent for walk-ins. Estimate that each person will use about two plastic water glasses per day, so multiply the number above by 2.0

Question: How many in the room
Purpose: To pay caterer for lunch
Method: Two days before event a number is given to the caterer based upon: Number advanced registration, plus 10 percent for walk-ins. No-shows are assumed to offset complementary seats. The caterer then counts total number of ten person tables that are set, and subtracts the number of seats not-served an entree

Question: How many in the room
Purpose: Newspaper reporter
Method: Count number of people in three rows, one row from front, one from middle, one from back. Determine average number per row from sample of three. Walk down aisle and count number of rows. Multiple average per row, times number of rows. That number is close enough for his purpose"

Dr. Deming has made his point clear: Change the test and you get a new answer. To say that moisture content is to be less than 4 percent has no meaning if we do not specify the method of measurement. One method yields less than 4 percent. Another method yields more than 4 percent. Contract disagreements often arise from the lack of a complete operational definition. I must review our procedures and contracts to make sure we use operational definitions.

Misunderstandings Are Often Caused by the Lack of Operational Definitions

A label reads,

50% Wool.

What does this mean? How would we operationally define 50 percent wool?

A lack of operational definitions often causes misunderstandings between people. We can often observe conflicts between companies and between departments about allegedly defective parts, or allegedly malfunctioning apparatus. Their failure to state their requirements as an operational definition causes the conflicts. An operational definition includes: **criteria, test, and decision.**

"Here is a blanket that is 50 percent wool and 50 percent cotton. (Laughter)

"Step #1: Define the test method.

"To test a blanket, cut ten holes, each 15 mm in diameter. Select the holes by finding location centers by random numbers. We number the holes 1 to 10. Next, hand the samples to a chemist for testing. He weighs the sample, dissolves the components in a specified caustic solution following prescribed rules. He filters the solution, dries the filtrate, weighs and records the result for each of the ten samples. He computes the average of the ten proportions.

"Step #2: Develop criteria.

"A criterion is neither right nor wrong: it is merely a rule agreed upon in advance. We could choose any number of criteria. For instance, we could decide that 50 percent wool means that the average of ten combined samples is equal to or more than 50 percent wool. If we apply this criterion, the blanket in the diagram is acceptable.

"However, if we want samples to have 'about the same amount' of wool throughout the blanket we might adapt another criterion:

$$\overline{X} \geq 50\%$$
$$X_{MAX} - X_{MIN} \leq 0.02\%$$

This means that the difference between the highest and lowest test value is less than or equal to 0.02 percent

"Step #3: Make a decision.

If we are buying a single blanket we will merely trust the label in our favorite store. However, if we are manufacturing blankets, or buying them for a hotel or cruise ship, we need this operational definition. We agree with purchasing agent in advance to a test and criterion(a)."

All Wool

All Cotton

Reflections on Operational Definitions

As I sit in my hotel room I think back thirty years ago to college. It seems that somewhere in my past I've heard of operational definitions.

Yes, I can remember my first year at college. I was taking a first-level science course, something like "Introduction to Physics." I remember my confusion because high-school physics was all about pulleys and levers but college physics was the philosophy of science.

I remember the lecture hall. I sat among hundreds of other first year students. The course focused on operational definitions, measurement, and the scientific method. Practically the same themes taught in Dr. Deming's theory of Profound Knowledge.

Yet in business we use operational definitions without really knowing what we are doing. Our finance people look at numbers all the time without investigating their meaning. We have numbers, and if we print these numbers on computer paper, they take on reality. They become truth.

The computer says we have 107 six-inch bronze butterfly valves in inventory. But what is the operational definition of "107 six-inch bronze butterfly valves in

inventory?" Does this mean a man or woman, on a certain day, counted that many valves? Does it mean the valves are all in the same bin? Or does it mean that for the past six months the computer has been adding and subtracting inventory levels since the last actual count? What about returns? Are all the valves operational?

Next we ask, "What is the purpose of our research?" Are we asking to figure out the amount to pay on inventory tax? Or are we asking so we can ship to a customer in the field? If a critical customer should call and tell us that he needs 52 six-inch bronze butterfly valves for immediate delivery, I use an operational definition that includes a procedure for counting. Someone walks to the bin, counts, tags, and ships 52 six-inch bronze butterfly valves. If we are doing an estimate for reordering, I may be content with the number on the computer report.

So operational definitions go to the heart of almost all business decisions and business communications. I've often had to sort through a discussion between departments in which the opening salvo is "their paperwork is always wrong." I usually

Now with what I have learned here I can teach my people to develop criteria, conduct tests, and make decisions. I wonder what Dr. Deming has in store for us next?

make each party sit down and describe their complaints in enough detail to show where they are not communicating. I never quite realized I was developing operational definitions.

DAY THREE

11

Management of People
Leadership, and Training

The Job of the Manager of People

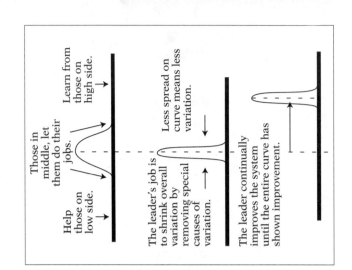

Those in middle, let them do their jobs.

Learn from those on high side.

Help those on low side.

The leader's job is to shrink overall variation by removing special causes of variation.

Less spread on curve means less variation.

The leader continually improves the system until the entire curve has shown improvement.

D r. Deming continues his lecture after the Day 4 morning presentations are completed. "The aim of leadership is to improve the performance of man and machine, to improve quality, to increase output, and simultaneously to bring pride of workmanship to people.

"Put in a negative way, the aim of leadership is not merely to find and record failures of people, but to remove causes of failure: to help people to do a better job with less effort."

Fifteen years ago I had a boss who was sincere. She did her best, but had the unique ability to get the staff painfully upset. She was brilliant and knew more about the total program than anyone else. Sitting around her large circular conference table, we each reported in our turn. She quizzed us about the programs, the customers, the regulations, the budgets, and the performance levels, and invariably she would find our weaknesses. Then she switched off her charm. We called her meetings the Star Chamber, named aptly for some silly movie of violence and mayhem.

The staff reacted to avoid her punishment. We sanitized the information. Each

staffer calculated the spin to put on the numbers, to position his or her reports in the best light. She did not achieve her goal of improvement of the process since each staffer twisted reality in an attempt to escape unscathed. The result was management by fear. The results in the short run were not bad. We made the right numbers no matter by what method. However, we could have done much more with a manager who was more of a leader, and less of an inquisitor.

After a few years, the staff got even. We repaid the years of frustration and fear with an all-out rebellion. We supported a new manager in a great bureaucratic battle, a modern day tribal combat. The cost to the system was unknown and unknowable.

Today I learned that a manger of people has three major aims. The first aim is to learn, by calculation or otherwise, who, if anyone, lies outside the system. Those outside the system on the negative side need special help. We can learn from those outside the system on the positive side.

A second responsibility is to improve consistency of performance of the vast majority who are within the system, so that apparent differences between people continually diminish.

The third responsibility is to improve the system continually, so everybody can do a better job with greater satisfaction.

Why a Leader Must Be a Trainer

Dr. Deming refers back to Day 2 to suggest the leader's job be to know whom to train and whom not to train. How can one know? On page 73, Dr. Deming covered the case of the golfer who used his scores to track his performance on the links. From this example we learned the theory that if a worker is not in statistical control, training helps to improve the worker's performance. Once a worker reaches statistical control based on the worker's data alone, additional training contributes nothing to his performance. To gain improvement in the latter case we must make a basic change to the system. One possible basic change is to transfer the worker to another task.

I heard of a use of this principle for bank tellers. After a two-to-three week training period, the new teller works in a branch. At the end of each day, the teller accounts for all of the transactions. From time to time, the transactions do not balance. This is called "Teller Differences."

Several banks measure the number of differences and their value. All tellers experience some differences. The nature of the differences depends on the type of work processed at the particular branch. By measuring the performance of tellers within a branch, it is possible to find those whose differences represent special causes.

They plot on a control chart the difference data for tellers identified as having more than normal differences. If the chart shows special causes the teller returns to teller school for further training. If the chart shows a stable system of differences, they transfer the teller to another position.

Before lessons performance is unstable, erratic. Many points are outside the control limits.

After lessons, performance is stable, predictable to some degree. All points are within the control limits. The average has gone down substantially (in golf the low score wins).

— Upper Control Limit (UCL) $\bar{\bar{X}} + 3\hat{\sigma}$†

— Lower Control Limit (LCL) $\bar{\bar{X}} - 3\hat{\sigma}$

Lessons are given

Before lessons performance is stable.

Lessons are given

After lessons, performance is stable. When a person is already in statistical control, training does no good. Improvements come from changing the system.

†Reads: "x double bar plus three sigma hat." This means: "the grand average plus three times the estimated standard deviation."

Dr. Deming says that we have only one chance to train a person correctly. He is referring to the theory that once a person has learned a task so that their performance is consistent, that person does not benefit from further training. The habits, good or bad, are fixed in that person.

The Leader's Job Is to Know When Statistical Stability Has Been Reached

I realize that as a manager of people it is my job to know when my processes are in statistical control. How can I tell? When all the points in a control chart of the process fall randomly within the upper and lower control limits. I like to call it "knowing when my process is stable." I now see that stability applies to people, work groups, departments, procedures, services, processes, and equipment. It applies to just about everything. It is like a law of nature applied to the workplace.

The payoff is that if my process is stable, I can make some fairly confident predictions about the future. I am reasonably sure that performance will continue within the control limits and that can help me set prices, set staffing levels, set production levels, etc.

If the process is not in control, then I am in a state of chaos, constant emergencies, complaining customers, morale problems, fluctuations in product quality that no one can understand, on and on. We make money even in a state of chaos, in spite of ourselves. Sometimes we discover a market need, fill the need, make money, surrounded by chaos, only to lose the market share as others with stable systems come into the market.

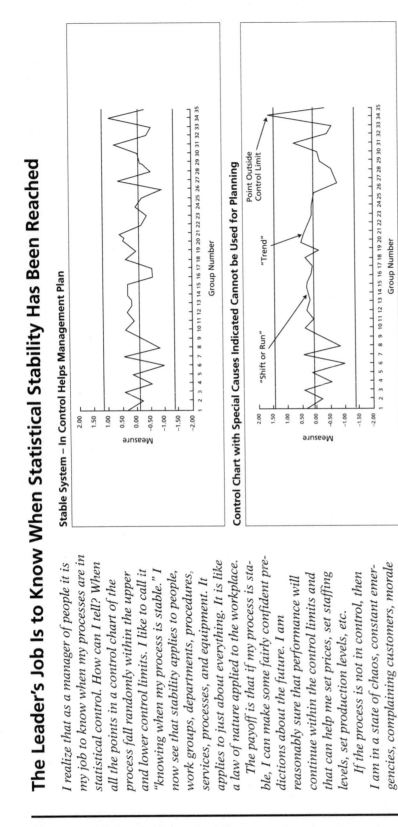

Stable System – In Control Helps Management Plan

Measure / Group Number

Control Chart with Special Causes Indicated Cannot be Used for Planning

"Shift or Run" "Trend" Point Outside Control Limit

Measure / Group Number

The tough question is how can I as the leader tell when the process is in statistical control? The answer is to use the control chart. The control chart was the invention of Dr. Walter Shewhart (see pages 98–99 and 148–149). Dr. Deming is now discussing the use of a control chart in several applications. One of these was by Dr. Sugiyama who figured out the time of full rehabilitation of a patient (see page 131). Dr. Sugiyama wanted to give the patient all the help that would do him any good but not waste effort. The control chart provided a solution to this dilemma.

The Manager's Job Is to Know the Difference between Random Causes and Special Causes of Variation

I understand that a good manager can tell the difference between special and common causes of variation to solve problems systematically. The way to tell them apart is with a control chart. We compute a control chart with mathematical formulas. Do I know enough math?

It turns out to be simpler than interpreting a financial statement. Dr. Deming shows some clever and simple ways of determining if a process is stable or unstable. For instance, Dr. Deming described a manager of people who runs a department of welders. Often we have data on hand. Here our available data are as follows:

Welder	Number of Faults per 5,000 Welds
1	8
2	15
3	10
4	4
5	7
6	24
7	8
8	8
9	10
10	3
11	8
Total =	105

Welder Performance

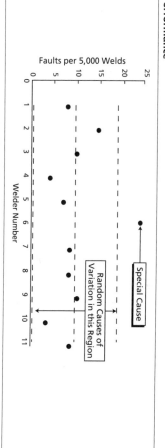

Who, if anyone, is performing worse than the rest? Is it Welder 6? How about Welder 2? Should we consider Welders 3 and 9 as substandard? To find out who, if anyone, differs from the rest, Dr. Deming constructs a control chart. There are several types of control charts. The appendix discusses different types of charts. Here, a c-chart is best.

The center line of the c-chart = Average = 105 /11 = 9.55 faults in 5000 welds.

The control limits are computed from the data in the table at the right.

$$\left.\begin{array}{l} UCL \\ LCL \end{array}\right\} = 9.55 \pm 3\sqrt{9.55} = \left\{\begin{array}{l} 19.0 \\ 0 \end{array}\right.$$

Welder 6's work is outside the system and in need of individual attention. Perhaps the stream of work received by Welder 6 is more difficult,

or perhaps his equipment is faulty. The manager of the welders must find out what causes Welder 6 to have so many flaws. He examines the process to see what contributes to the excess flaws. It may be a physical matter. Welder 6 may need glasses or a new prescription. It is the manager's task to get to the bottom of the problem and help Welder 6 to become more effective.

The system may still be producing an average of 8 faulty welds for 5,000 welds. The manager may wish for further improvements. Armed with this control chart, the manager now knows that the workers are a stable part of the process. To make improvements manipulation of the workers will probably achieve little. The leader must look beyond the workers, examine the equipment, the procedures, the job itself, to achieve meaningful improvement.

The Manager's Job Is to Dig—To Learn What Is Going On

People will not tell the manager their troubles freely. They may not know how to describe the problem. They may not realize that there is a problem. When they do talk to the manager, the manager may not understand the worker or may not listen.

Dr. Deming tells a story in which managers conduct "hands-on research" to identify those needing special help. The manager of a trucking company spent two days with each driver. One may say he should have been doing it all along but he was not.

His purpose was to learn the difficulties of city drivers, and to treat trucking as a process for improvement. After returning from a trip with Jim, the manager was very excited. Jim had for years been a problem driver. He would return late each day. His efficiency rating was the lowest of all drivers. Although he appeared hard working, his score was usually the lowest, he was below average. They wanted to fire him long ago, but somehow just kept him on.

The manager learned, from his short field visit, that Jim's territory was behind a range of high hills. The company-issued radio was useless in the circumstances; the hills interfered with transmission. Jim regularly drove several miles to a spot that gave him a clear line to the dispatcher's antenna so he could hear his pickup instructions. Management solved the problem by giving Jim rolls of quarters and instructions to phone several times each day to receive the dispatcher's instructions.

One may say the fault is Jim's. Why did he not complain? Why did he not stop using the radio and start using the phone himself? Was it fear?

How will we ever know? He just wanted to do a good job, to do the best he could. He knew the company spent money for a radio and central antenna. Management had issued this radio and must know what it can and cannot do. He knew that others were using the system. He did not want to rock the boat! Jim was only doing his best.

Much is written about Management by Walking Around (MBWA). By itself it does

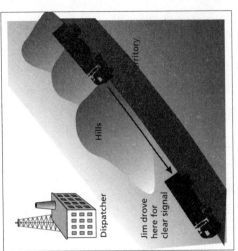

Dispatcher

Hills

Jim drove here for clear signal

...territory

For years driver performance was below average since hills blocked the transmission of radio signals.

very little. The manager must know what to do on his or her field visit. The manager does not only shake hands like a politician. To be effective, Dr. Deming suggests asking a simple question: "What gets in the way of your doing your job?" Then sit back and listen! And finally, act.

A Manager's Job Is to Dig—To See Who Needs Special Help

Dr. Deming again describes how a leader can discover and display information about system stability. Although control charts come in a variety of forms their interpretation is the same.

This is a case of a company that sorts grocery store coupons. Workers unpack coupons received from a food chain. Staples and rubber bands are removed. They sort the prepared coupons. The sorting units might do a primary (rough) or secondary (final) sort. Each sorter, men and women, has a workstation with 80 pigeon holes. There are approximately 30 workers in a sorter unit. There are approximately 240 workers in each of four plants. They use a random sample to inspect the work. Over a month, the inspectors find an average of 44 errors per 10,000 coupons.

The management used a special paper called Binomial Probability Paper (BIPP) to plot the results for each operator. The X-axis contained the number right, while the Y-axis contained the number of errors. The center line is the average for all operators,

44 defects per 10,000 observations. Using a scale on the paper, one can plot the upper and lower control limits. For more data about this method see Kaoru Ishikawa's *Guide To Quality Control*, Chapter 10.

While the bulk of the workers fell within the control limits, some workers were above the upper limit and some were below the lower limit. Those workers whose error rate places them above the upper control limit need special help. Some may need glasses. Other may be dyslexic requiring transfer to another job. One was too short and could not reach upper row of pigeonholes at her workstation. Management cut her trestle table down so she could reach her work.

Those whose error rates fall below the lower control limit are also worth study. Are their numbers correct? If yes, do they have easier work than the others? Do they have some skill that, if taught to everyone, could increase the total quality of the group? What makes them so much better?

The manager of people uses tools such as this control chart to understand

his or her process. The manager's job is to work with the group above the upper control limit to get them to be as good as those within the limits. The manager studies those below the lower control limit to learn improved methods. Management then applies these across the board. Finally, the manager takes steps to make the total process better. This requires a basic change in one or more of the elements of the process. It is of interest to note that the management team that accomplished this consisted mostly of people who had had a fourth-grade education or less.

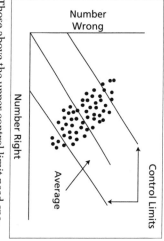

Those above the upper control limit need special help. Those below the lower control limit can teach us. Those within the control limits should be left alone.

DAY FOUR

The Manager's Job Is to Understand Inspection

Dr. Deming warns the group that faulty inspection will cause severe problems. It will frustrate the workers, cause us to misinterpret points on the control chart, and allow faulty product to get to the consumer. He illustrates his point with a situation where four inspectors inspect the work of seventeen operators. The work of the seventeen operators is allotted to the four inspectors by using random numbers. This will ensure that each operator has the same chance of being inspected by each of the four inspectors.

From a tested table of random numbers, or from a tested random number generator, select a four-digit random number. If the number is 0409, the next item from worker 9 goes to inspector 4. The first two digits are the inspector number, the last two digits are the operator number. If the number is 6438, we disregard it.

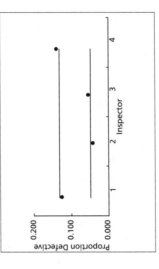

1 2 3 4 5 6 7 8 9 10 11 12 13 14 15 16 17
Worker Number

Inspector Number

1   2   3   4

What do the data suggest, if anything? You might look to see which of the workers is producing the most defects. It seems clear:
Operator 8 produced 14 defects
Operator 11 produced 27 defects
Operator 17 produced 36 defects

These three operators produced 77 defects (14 + 27 + 36 = 77). Just three operators produced almost half of all the defects. If I use the c-chart formula, these three would all be

Worker	Inspector 1	2	3	4	All
1	1	0	0	3	4
2	2	0	0	3	5
3	0	1	1	4	6
4	3	2	2	2	9
5	7	0	0	0	7
6	0	0	0	1	1
7	1	1	1	4	7
8	3	2	3	6	14
9	2	1	0	0	3
10	1	1	1	0	3
11	9	3	5	10	27
12	3	1	0	1	5
13	4	1	1	2	8
14	4	1	1	2	8
15	0	0	1	3	4
16	1	0	0	4	5
17	11	4	6	15	36
All	52	18	22	60	152
n	400	410	390	390	1590
p-bar	.130	.044	.056	.154	.096

and the number found defective. We can simply calculate the proportion that was found defective as 52/400 = .130.

It is obvious that the inspectors get different results. Using a p-chart shows: Inspectors 1 and 4 are in close agreement (.130 and .154) and inspectors 2 and 3 are also in close agreement (.044 and .056). However, each pair of inspectors substantially disagrees with the other pair of inspectors.

Faulty Inspection
Inspector 1 and 4 agree and 2 and 3 agree. There is no system of inspection.

outside the control limits. These are the ones who need special help. Well, we would call this a theory. Our theory is that three operators are a special cause of variation. The answer is simple, one any manager can see: retrain these three operators. Right? Wrong!

Stop for a moment. Remember we are searching for system stability. The system consists of operators, equipment, management, and inspection. Let us examine the stability of the inspection process. We have data on the number of items inspected by each inspector,

Something is unusual. The inspection process itself is out of control. Perhaps the inspectors follow different procedures, or have different operational definitions or different equipment. So as managers we must dig into all aspects of our system, like detectives looking for causes of variation. We definitely need an operational definition so that the variation between the inspectors can be reduced, otherwise the employees will be frustrated.

The Manager's Job Is to Drive Out Fear So That Control Systems Work Properly

We need knowledge about the process, whether stable or not, to decide how to go about making improvement. This knowledge comes from the measurement of the system. The system of measurement is a part of the process. The measurement system contributes to the common causes of variation. It can also contribute special causes of variation. If people are afraid, the fear affects measurement. Dr. Deming uses real-life data to illustrate this situation.

In the control chart the data points hug the 8.8 percent average line. It is unusual with so many points to see such a narrow distribution around the average. Dr. Deming investigated this condition with Dr. Chambers. They finally learned that there was a rumor throughout the plant. The rumor had it that if the percentage defect in the final audit ever reached 10 percent, the manager would "sweep the place out." The inspector believed the rumor. Consequently she never reported more than 22 defects out of her daily sample of 225. She thought that she was saving 300 jobs. She may well have caused the

loss of these jobs by reporting doctored numbers.

Fear caused the reporting of bad data. It did not matter whether the rumor was true or not. Since the inspector believed it, and acted on it, the effect was present. Dr. Deming tells that a new manager replaced the incumbent and alleviated the fear. Presumably he also improved the process.

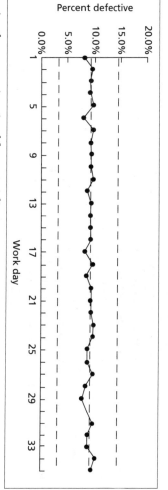

Percent defective

Hugging the average is a signal for a special cause of variation. Management's job is to investigate this signal.

The Manager's Job Is to Drive Out Fear

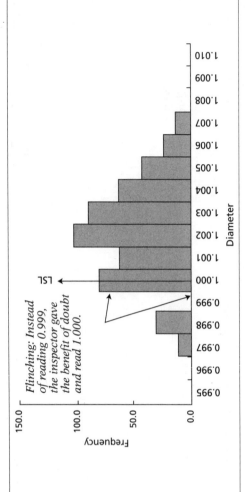

Flinching: Instead of reading 0.999, the inspector gave the benefit of doubt and read 1.000.

The histogram of measurements at the right shows a similar problem to the one cited on the previous page. An inspector measures the diameter of 500 parts and records his measurements. The line with the arrow is the lower specification limit (LSL). Items on or above this point are acceptable. Those less than 1.000 inch in diameter are too small to use. Note that there is a perceptible gap just below the LSL at 0.999 inches. Also notice that the frequency bar at the border, 1.000, is unusually high. From the shape of the distribution, we would have expected some items of 0.999 inch diameters. This is a symptom of "flinching."

There are several possibilities:

1. The inspector is trying to protect the people who make the part. This is similar to the example on the previous page. Fear that co-workers might lose their jobs makes the inspector classify doubtful items as good.

2. The inspector is afraid of his instruments. He lacks confidence that the readings are accurate. The same part may give more than one reading when he turns it. In case of a marginal reading, he assumes that the system of measurement is bad and gives the benefit of doubt to the part, accepting it.

3. The inspector is afraid of his own ability to use his instruments. The instruments are graduated only for each 0.002 of an inch. The inspector has to interpolate the odd readings. In case of doubt, the inspector will call a part good by classing it as 1.000 inch instead of 0.999 inch. A part 0.998 inch is clearly too small.

Reflections on the Manager's Task

There is much material in the last section to ponder. This is not what I learned in business school.

In business school we learned financial analysis: how to look at numbers, or so I thought. It didn't seem to matter much what business or industry we were examining. We learned many of the wrong things. I understand that some business schools, such as Fordham's Graduate School of Business, today teach the principles that Dr. Deming is teaching us here. I wish I had gone there.

Dr. Deming gives us the framework for a modern method of management. He expects us to dig below the superficial level. He expects us to use statistical tools to find who is within and who is without the system. Most people fall within the limits of normal skills. Occasionally someone will seem so good that their achievement falls outside the control limits. If the data are correct, and the person is doing the same work as the others, then we examine the performance to learn what made them so effective. If possible, we would like to teach the rest of the group this new method to improve everyone's effectiveness.

Those who fall outside the limits on the "bad" side need special help. As a manager of people, it is my job to learn why their performance is outside the system's achievement. Perhaps I did not train them properly, or train them sufficiently. Perhaps they cannot do the task I set for them. In either case, it is my responsibility as manager to help these people. If they cannot do the work, I must transfer them to some task they can do.

The others are to be left alone. They are doing as well as the system will allow. If I want improvement of those in statistical control, I must make a basic improvement of the entire system.

Life used to be so simple, yet really more bizarre. I just calculated the average of a series of measurements or evaluations. Then by stamping my feet, making speeches, and telling those below average that they are below average, I let them know that they better shape up and get themselves above average.

I now see how ludicrous this thinking was. By definition, half the people will be above the average and half will be below. To rant and rave that those below average should be above is just as stupid as to compliment those above average. They are all just part of the same system. Some happen to be on top now, others happen to be on the bottom. Hundreds of factors, out-side their individual control, make up this circumstance. Rather than stir up people, the manager's job is to see the entire system. It's like the difference between seeing the forest and seeing the trees. Some trees will be taller, some will be shorter. Some above average, some below average, but they are all part of a forest. There's no sense in punishing some or rewarding others. If, however, we see one tree that is outside the control limits, we might want to examine this tree more closely.

The other management technique drilled into me in school was management by objective (MBO). My fundamental leadership method was MBO. I wonder how much damage I did through the use of MBO. I will never know.

Someone at the seminar circulated an article from the Washington Post that read: "The Bush administration is dusting off an approach that President Nixon brought to Washington: 'management by objectives' or MBO. President Bush sent a memo this week to Cabinet secretaries and chiefs to 'give this MBO effort your personal attention.'" At the Deming seminar we all had a good laugh at Washington, but secretly we all knew that our own companies are doing the same thing.

12

System of Measurement

Be Aware of the Hazards of False Consensus

Dr. Deming has shown the need for a system of measurement. He now discusses the potential harm of a faulty measurement system. He explains that just a few faulty observations about our process can change our theories, hunches, and beliefs. These errors, if undetected, can put us on the road to disaster.

Healthy Consensus: Consensus after everyone has a chance to speak his or her mind and to ask questions, all without fear, benefits the entire team.

Unhealthy Consensus: Consensus in inspection or anywhere else that may only mean that one person has intellectually overpowered the others, and the consensus is one opinion, with others silently acquiescing.

I sense he is suggesting that we search for knowledge that can serve society better, and he who better serves society will earn a profit. Society is willing to pay a profit to any organization that serves them.

As managers we use inspection to make and record our observations, we develop a system of measurement. We should expect differences between inspectors.

Often I feel surrounded by "yes men." It seems that people try to figure out the prevailing opinions and then go with those. Sometimes I will hold back my opinion in the hope of smoking out what is on my subordinates' minds. Dr. Deming makes the distinction between healthy and unhealthy consensus.

Early in my career, I attended a meeting with a newly elected county executive. He asked us to speak our minds on a politically sensitive issue. I mentioned the federal funding to the SMSA. The executive stopped me and asked for a definition of the SMSA. Having just finished graduate school I thought everyone knew about Standard Metropolitan Statistical Areas (SMSA) defined by the 1970

Census. My respect for the executive went up. I suspect that most people would pretend to understand the abbreviation. This honest exchange of information gave me confidence to state my opinions on a politically unpopular issue. So instead of being surrounded by "yes men," the elected official encouraged healthy exchange by asking relevant questions, even risking asking a "stupid question."

Independent versus Dependent Inspection

Dr. Deming continues to illustrate his points with real-life situations. Two doctors, an older

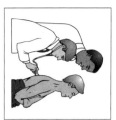

and a younger, make rounds together. They discuss each patient and, through consensus, decide if the patient is better, the same, or worse. Sounds like a good system, right?

Wrong. Through this type of consensus the opinion of the more senior doctor often becomes the opinion of both. The younger doctor may be dependent upon the older for promotional opportunities or other benefits. The relationship between the two is at stake if the younger disagrees too often.

I recall a news article about pilots and copilots. Apparently someone studied recorded conversation recovered from crashes. The researchers theorized that copilots too often deferred to pilots. Copilots are dependent upon pilots to rack up flying hours, they often know little of each other before an assigned flight, and they follow a rigid command tradition. The researchers observed that con-

sensus was usually the pilot's opinion: The copilots may have hinted at a problem, ("look at all that snow coming down") but did not speak their minds openly.

Dr. Deming suggests a simple solution for using doctors to inspect the patients. Each doctor records his or her opinion separately after examining a patient. The results, plotted in an easy-to-read chart, show when they agree and when they disagree.

We would expect some disagreements. Then from time to time they would compare notes, ask questions of each other and learn from each other.

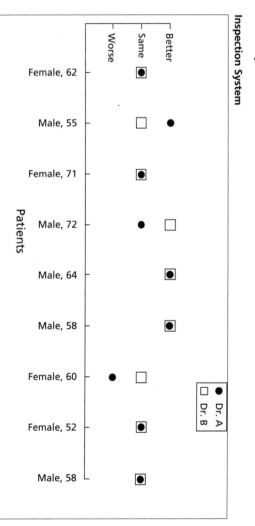

Inspection System

Patients

Better / Same / Worse

Female, 62
Male, 55
Female, 71
Male, 72
Male, 64
Male, 58
Female, 60
Female, 52
Male, 58

● Dr. A
□ Dr. B

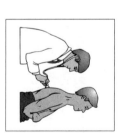

Measurement Requires Operational Definition to Be Useful

Apparently, if we wish to avoid undue influence in the case of the two doctors rating patients, they must examine the patients independently. However, even if the doctors agree when making independent diagnosis, it does not mean that their diagnosis is necessarily "right." An interesting question is, "What is right?"

The agreement of the two doctors only means that they have an internally consistent and repeatable measurement system. They have a system of measurement. It has nothing to do with them being "right."

What is a "correct" judgment, what is "right?" From the system of Profound Knowledge we know that there is no correct or incorrect, there is no true value. There is only a value decided by a particular operational definition of measurement. Recalling the discussion on the first day of the value of inventory, we found that changing the method of measurement results in a different inventory value.

What is 1 centimeter, what is 1 kilogram? Time—how do we measure time? There are accepted international

definitions for the CGS (Centimeter, Gram, Second) system. We define our own inch pound system in terms of the CGS system.

I now understand the insistence of Dr. Deming that we must understand the purpose of our measurements. For airlines schedules, the closest minute is OK. For a national TV network, measurement is finer, by the second or even tenth of a second, (9:00 A.M. means 8:59 plus 59 seconds then start the commercial). For sports and the Olympics, measurements often are in the hundredths of a second. Every measurement needs an operational definition. Imagine running a modern business without operational definitions, or even without the idea of operational definitions.

Operational definition is an idea we miss so often. We look at measurements and invest time and energy in analysis of numbers as though they were "right," without variation. Then we make important decisions based upon these numbers. We spend little or no time and energy understanding the method of measurement, the operational definition. If the numbers come on computer paper, we accept them without question.

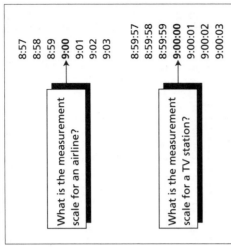

What does 9 o'clock mean?

What is the measurement scale for an airline?

	8:57
	8:58
	8:59
→	**9:00**
	9:01
	9:02
	9:03

What is the measurement scale for a TV station?

	8:59:57
	8:59:58
	8:59:59
→	**9:00:00**
	9:00:01
	9:00:02
	9:00:03

Know Your Data

As a young man I worked in an organization that had an MBO system for reporting client services. Our supervisors would not let us go to lunch on Fridays until we submitted our weekly service reports. Each worker would go down the list of clients, checking boxes to show the type of service provided. There was no training in the use of the checklist, nor any checks of how we scored the reports. Neither was there consistency in language or in level of services offered. This was just a task to do before lunch on Friday. Incidentally, service on Friday afternoon, one tenth of the weekly total, was the result of a guess. It made no difference because the rest of the week's figures were also guesses.

The supervisor was pleased that she had her reports in by end of the day Friday. Management was pleased, because all supervisors complied.

Two years later I was on a corporate study team. Being the youngest to join the team, I was astounded to find Ph.D-level social psychologists gathered around a table having a serious discussion about the service performance data. It was their job to analyze the data and prepare a report to management. I listened for two hours as they examined the data and discussed the sophisticated statistical analysis they would perform. Sheepishly I raised my hand to explain I had worked in the field, and had dutifully contributed each Friday afternoon to the numbers before them. I told them of the methodology we followed. They learned about the variation, the haphazard nature of the data collection, the lack of training, and the absence of checks of any type. The Ph.D.'s were sad. Suddenly, they knew their plans for analysis would be meaningless and potentially misleading.

Measurement Requires a Holistic View

A department store manager, just trying to do his best, developed a campaign to improve sales. The clerks, just trying to do their best, worked hard to sell more merchandise.

The clerk improved her sales quite well. She was on a commission basis. Psychologists say that commissions increase sales. And it did.

The only problem was that commissions also increased returns. The star clerk increased her sales by encouraging people to "Take it home and try it on." Too late management discovered that her returns were also high. What does it cost a department store to handle a return?

The cost to process returns on average is $28 each. The manager had a wonderful idea to increase sales, and it did increase sales, but the total organization suffered.

In my company we make this mistake regularly. The sales department will sell a product or service that we can't deliver profitably. The sales people make their numbers look good, but operations can't deliver. When we try to sort it out it becomes

an exercise in blaming one another. Dr. Deming calls this suboptimization.

When one part of a company does well, by optimizing itself, the entire organization may suffer. (It usually does.) Each unit optimizing itself without regard to the other units results in suboptimization of the entire system. As in football, the fastest runner isn't always the best. If he runs too fast he will outrun his blockers.

Now I realize that this happens in my company. One department will make great

numbers. They will get rewarded. For example, purchasing will lower the cost of incoming materials, but those in the plant will complain at the extra work needed to use this material. The extra costs in the plant are unknown and unknowable. My job is to know what is going on, to examine cost to the entire system, and to avoid looking at costs only at the department-by-department level.

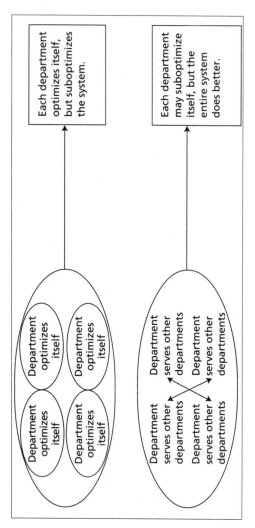

Each department optimizes itself, but suboptimizes the system.

Each department may suboptimize itself, but the entire system does better.

The Need to Look at the Measurement over Time

Dr. Deming reads from a church bulletin, "We need a new roof. This year we need a special donation . . ." Yes, there is a problem this year. The roof is leaking. But the problem has been around for over a decade. It is not the only long-term problem in the church. To see some of the problems, write out on a slip of paper:

- The revenues each year for ten years,
- The membership each year for ten years, and
- The expenses each year for ten years.

In a minute you will see a long-term trend. Dr. Deming explained that the church had been in a decline for more than a decade. The members are getting older. New members are not joining. The solution is not just a new roof.

Perhaps Dr. Deming is talking about his own church. We can imagine a church with an older population. If the church is in a city, then the suburban growth over many years pulled potential members to the suburbs. A look at the numbers over ten years shows the trend.

It is so obvious and so simple. Look for long-term trends over time. Yet in American business we just can't seem to look beyond the last two or three quarters. Instead of looking at numbers over a long trend of ten years, we look at the last three quarters. No one even has the numbers for the last ten years. Managers get transferred to another department and data get lost. Nobody keeps the important numbers. We can't find numbers that far back. So we focus on the short run, we see the trees but not the forest.

As a boss I have, for years, felt the need to step back, to remove myself from day-to-day crises to look over the horizon into the future. Simultaneously, I have to look into the past in a way that makes sense. Constancy of purpose, understanding the past, planning for the future, developing a system of measurement that truly helps the company survive and prosper: that is my job, the job of the executive.

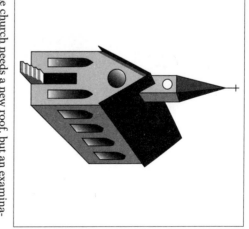

The church needs a new roof, but an examination of membership data shows a steady ten-year decline.

13

Closing Thoughts

DAY FOUR   DAY THREE   DAY TWO   DAY ONE

Service Organizations

Improvement in America's standard of living is highly dependent on better quality and productivity in the service sector.

Dr. Deming explains, "Figures published by the Census show that 75 out of 100 people are employed in service organizations.

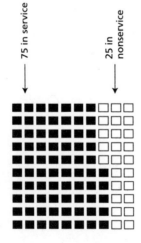

75 in service

25 in nonservice

"If we add to these figures the ones in manufacturing industries who provide support services, we find that 86 in 100 are engaged in service. This leaves only 14 out of 100 to make items that we can drive, use, misuse, drop, or break, and these 14 includes those in agriculture."

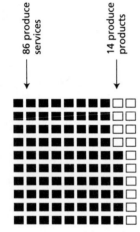

86 produce services

14 produce products

Dr. Deming gives us another important idea. Out of every group of 100 people working, only 14 actually produce something that "can fall on your foot," something that is a real product. Even in a manufacturing facility, most of the people are just producing services, not actual products. Yet so much of my energy goes into squeezing out the last penny from the manufacturing people. The comptroller's people, under my direction, have the mistaken attitude that any cost is too high. Now Dr. Deming is adding another dimension.

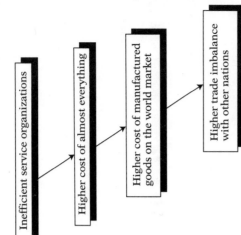

Inefficient service organizations

Higher cost of almost everything

Higher cost of manufactured goods on the world market

Higher trade imbalance with other nations

I must also focus my energies toward improvement on the service side of my business. Well, of course, it makes sense, but what do I do? Do these same principles apply to services? Can you actually do a control chart of a service function? Can I find both common and special causes when it comes to service?

Dr. Deming's Theory Applies to Service Organizations

> All that we have learned about the system of Profound Knowledge, 14 Obligations of management, and the Deadly Diseases also applies to a service organization.

Dr. Deming shows that the principles and methods for improvement are the same for service as for manufacturing. Actual applications differ from one product to another, and from one type of service to another, just as manufacturing concerns differ from one to another.

An early paper on achieving quality in a service sector is by W. Edwards Deming and Leon Geoffrey, published in 1941.[1] Although Shewhart entitled his first book *Economic Control of Quality of Manufactured Product*, he, Deming, and others recognized quickly that his theory applied to the service sector as well. The Census Bureau has recognized the application of this theory to its work. As early as the Depression, Morris H. Hansen applied sample theory in the

Census. Later, as head of the Census, he encouraged the use of the method discussed here to control the quality of the work. The Census Bureau did some fine work in achieving quality in a service application.

I sense that Dr. Deming has prepared a pathway to lead us to what we must do. He marks this path with sign posts, clues, maps, and inspiration. He got my attention with the numbers of people in the service sector. I ask myself, "Does what we learned apply to service and to manufacturing?" Then just as my question forms Dr. Deming answers it. He is a guide taking me through a four-day journey into the

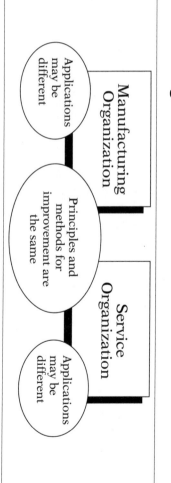

Manufacturing Organization

Applications may be different

Principles and methods for improvement are the same

Service Organization

Applications may be different

very essence of science applied to the everyday workplace. The stakes are high. The future of my company, the jobs of my people are in the balance.

[1] Deming, W. Edwards and Leon Geoffry, "On Sample Inspection in the Processing of Census Returns," *Journal of the American Statistical Association*, Vol. 36, September 1941, pp. 351–360.

Costly Misunderstandings

Dr. Deming says, "Common to manufacturing and any service organization is that mistakes and defects are costly. The further a mistake goes without correction, the greater the cost of correcting it. The cost of a defect that reaches the consumer may be the costliest, but no one knows what this cost is. It is unknown and unknowable."

Under the theory of Frederick W. Taylor, management obtains quality by prescribing a procedure to follow and ensuring that the clerks and lower level managers follow this procedure rigorously. There is an unstated assumption in most service organizations that we have fully defined and followed procedures. Yet in practice this is often not the condition. The lessons of the red beads make it clear that the most rigorous adherence to procedures does not ensure the desired quality. If the process is poor, no amount of adherence to procedure can help.

Management tries to protect itself with a series of inspectors. Obligation 3 described on pages 48 through 52 covers some problems associated with inspection. Most of the inspection in service applications is of the dependent variety, the least effective. Dependent inspection reviews the work after it has been completed. Many service organizations are taking advantage of the computer to move to independent inspection. The work is done twice and then compared by computer. While this method has some advantage over the dependent method, it is not the best solution. If the two pieces of work disagree, which is correct? It is possible that neither is correct.

Service practitioners: cease dependence on mass inspection. Work on the process. If the process is fail-safe then the work will be good. As stated on page 52: inspect the process, not the product.

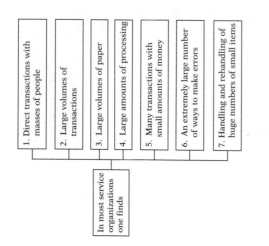

In most service organizations one finds

1. Direct transactions with masses of people

2. Large volumes of transactions

3. Large volumes of paper

4. Large amounts of processing

5. Many transactions with small amounts of money

6. An extremely large number of ways to make errors

7. Handling and rehandling of huge numbers of small items

Two Types of Quality

In both service and manufacturing there are two types of quality. First is quality of design, the ability to design products and services that customers want. Second is quality of delivery. This is our ability to produce products that meet the design. To achieve quality improvement, we need to consider both types of quality. We realize leverage of improvement by going upstream and improving the design.

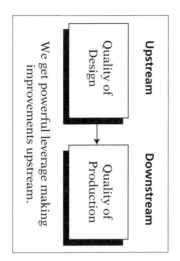

Upstream

Quality of Design

Downstream

Quality of Production

We get powerful leverage making improvements upstream.

This makes sense. We design a service; then we deliver that service. It is hoped that we base our design upon the customer voice. We design something that pleases the customer. Too often I think

that my company designs what pleases us, or what we think pleases customers.

After designing a service, we then deliver it. Dr. Deming is suggesting that we get more leverage if we go upstream and improve our design. It seems that, in my company, we spend much time and energy badgering our people who deliver services. We focus so much on the delivery that we often forget that there is a design.

Our current customer research is usually of little help as we design a service. Do we really need research to tell us customers want fast, accurate, and friendly service? No, we need an in-depth type of customer research that really digs into what customers want and shows us root customer needs.

My bank recently surveyed me. They asked me about the friendliness of tellers, and about how I felt going to the bank. At no point in the survey was I asked about the confusing format for their monthly reconciliation statement.

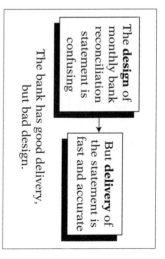

The **design** of monthly bank reconciliation statement is confusing

The bank has good delivery, but bad design.

But **delivery** of the statement is fast and accurate

I maintain checking accounts at two banks. At one bank the reconciliation statement is easy to read, easy to understand; therefore, the account balances more easily. At the bank that recently surveyed me, the statement is confusing. I have repeatedly mixed up numbers and felt frustrated when balancing that account. I won't use their automatic loan options because once I got so bogged down balancing the account that I'll never borrow money from them again. In the survey there was no way for me to explain my frustration. They never asked.

This is an example of a bank delivering friendly service, but it has not designed a reconciliation statement friendly to the user.

Improvement in Performance in a Bank

"Improving performance is not hard if you have a theory and a method. Bill Latzko, at the Irving Trust Company, had both a theory and a method. The bank was concerned with the large number of mistakes that were going to the customers. Mr. Latzko came up with the notion that if the bank made no mistakes, none would go to the customer."

Dr. Deming asked Mr. Latzko to tell his story to the audience. This is what he said:

The theory was to look at the process rather than the outcomes. The method was a control chart along with a participatory management style. The control chart is the process speaking to us. The use of the control chart is to identify and remove special causes of variation. Once one eliminates the special causes of variation, it is possible to work on the process to improve it.

Previously, when rejection rates went up, computer operators began blaming each other. Shift would react against shift and department against department. In the end everyone would blame "the machine." The results were discord, disharmony, and low morale. With statistical methods, one can automatically trace the reason for an abnormal rejection rate. Statistical methods identify the problem and tell management what type of action to take. With such a philosophy, everyone works together to improve the process.

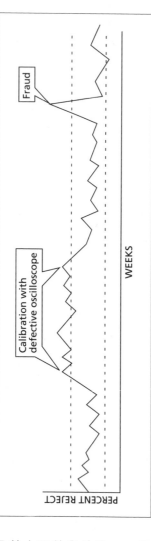

The banking system reads checks by means of magnetically encoded numbers (MICR) on the bottom 5/8th inch of the check. If the machine fails to read any digit after 75 tries, it rejects the check. Rejected checks cost a great deal of effort to reconcile and reenter. In addition, it was found that rejected checks were often further mishandled, causing great loss to the bank.

Rejects were monitored daily. The bank constructed an $\overline{X}$, R-chart at the end of each week using the average and range for the week. When a long series of points suddenly started to track the upper limit instead of the average, an investigation showed that the field engineer's oscilloscope, used for preventive maintenance, was not calibrated correctly. After adjustment of the oscilloscope, the process reverted to its normal low level of rejects.

Another example occured when the reject rate increased to such an extent that it was a special cause of variation. Immediate examination of the rejected checks revealed that a large number had plain, nonmagnetic ink. All these checks were for the same amount and payee. The quick discovery of the fraud enabled the bank to take fast action that led to the recovery of the funds.

When the purchasing department changed the supplier of magnetic ink ribbons for the encoding machine, they saved 10 percent of the cost. However, the new ribbons broke easily. The operators re-threaded the ribbons that broke. As the new ribbons phased into the system, the operators were re-threading more than encoding. Productivity fell dramatically. Investigation revealed the cause of the problem. The solution: Buy the old ribbons again.

Closing Thoughts

Dr. Shewhart's Discussion of Quality

"[The improvement of quality] is not so easy, and as soon as one feels fairly successful in the endeavor, he finds that the needs of the consumer have changed, competitors have moved in, there are new materials to work with, some better than the old ones, some worse; some cheaper than the old ones, some dearer."[2]

This is so true in my business and even in my personal purchases. I bought a stereo tape player, hooked it up and was thrilled with the sound quality. A loud click suddenly interrupted my reverie and startled me. The manufacturer designed the tape recorder so that at the end of the tape, the motor would shut off with a loud click. The click was disconcerting and annoying. So here was a product that pleased me in every way but one. Interestingly, I never bought anything with that brand name again.

The difficulty in defining quality is to translate **future needs of users** —— into ——▶ **measurable characteristics** —— so that ——▶ product can be **designed and built** to give **satisfaction** at a **price the user will pay.**

Following Shewhart's definition for this example, the manufacturer failed to translate customer needs into measurable characteristics. The customer's need was low mechanical sound. The manufacturer probably worked diligently to reduce motor noise while the tape was playing, but failed to follow the same discipline during shut off.

Customer Need	Measurable Characteristics	
Hear beautiful music, not mechanical noise	Mechanical noise during playing	Mechanical noise during shut off
	Very low mechanical noise	Loud click

Mr. Scherkenbach in his book, *The Deming Route*,[3] describes a method of figuring out measurable characteristics. The name of this method is **Quality Function Deployment (QFD). The method involves all areas responsible for producing and selling the final product. One finds a set of customer attributes, or desires, through research. Then one develops another set of planning requirements from the customer attributes. A matrix analysis matches these data to market conditions and resolves any potential conflicts. From the matrix analysis, a set of design target values evolves to guide the designers in producing a product that gives satisfaction at a price the customer is willing to pay.**

[2]Shewhart, Walter A., *The Economic Control of Quality of Manufactured Product* (Van Nostrand, 1931; reprinted American Society for Quality Control, 1980), Chapter 4.

[3]Scherkenbach, William W. *The Deming Route to Quality and Productivity*, (Washington, DC: George Washington University, CEE Press, 1986) p. 79 ff.

The Role of Consumer Research

> **"The purpose of studies in consumer preference is to adjust the product to the public, rather than as in advertising, to adjust the public to the product."**
>
> **(Irving Bross, _Design for Decision_ Macmillan, 1953, p. 95.)**

Why does my firm do consumer research? We use research to devise advertisements that persuade people to buy our products. Isn't there another purpose? Should we not try to adjust our product to the public?

Motorola was faced with the problem of trying to sell electronic paging devices to the Japanese market. The Japanese gave them detailed specifications for the product. Motorola was aghast at the reliability demanded by the Japanese. Convinced that this was merely an attempt to keep them out of the market, they checked the same devices made by the Japanese. To their surprise, they found that the Japanese product exceeded the specifications. This made them realize

that if they wanted to sell these devices to the Japanese, they would have to exceed the specifications. Motorola set about a long-term program to improve their methods. This allowed them to achieve the required quality.

In my company, customer research is the domain of the marketing department and the advertising folks. Rarely do the engineers get involved. Every year I fund a few studies for the R&D group, but small dollars compared to the big bucks for advertising testing. I wonder if we would need so much advertising if our products were designed better?

Consumer research is a process of communication between the manufacturer and potential users.

Dr. Deming is suggesting a new and more active role for the market research department. He sees them as setting up a communication process with customers, potential customers, and past customers to explore what they like and dislike about our products and services. He suggests that this process can be done reliably and eco-

nomically with sampling procedures and statistical methods.

Dr. Deming reminds us that the consumer cannot tell the supplier everything. Often the producer is in a far better position than the consumer to invent new designs and new services. Consumers never asked for an electric light, pneumatic tire, or fax machine.

The supplier, through his knowledge of the market, caused these innovations.

Analytic and Enumerative Studies—Why versus What

During the seminar, Dr. Deming discussed two instances of deciding the nature of a product. In one case the product consists of human beings: Two physicians find out whether a patient is better, the same, or worse (see page 177). The other case deals with deciding the grade of leather. Both cases are enumerative in nature. That means that we are finding a status of the product, not why it exists.

Dr. Deming has for years made the distinction between analytic and enumerative use of data. In an analytical study, we ask why something is the way we observe it so that we can take action. An enumerative study is what we observe: a specific condition or count. Dr. Deming treats this subject extensively in his book, *Some Theory of Sampling*, Chapter 7.

The illustration shown on this page came originally from an article Dr. Deming published in 1952. It illustrates the difference between enumerative and analytical sampling. The Supply Bowl contains red and white beads. We take an arbitrary amount from the Supply Bowl and place it in the Lot

Bowl. Then we draw a random sample from the Lot Bowl and place it in the Sample Bowl. In an enumerative analysis, we use the data from the sample bowl to estimate what is in the Lot Bowl. In an analytical problem, we try to estimate what is in the Supply Bowl from what is in the Sample Bowl. We do this to take action on the Supply Bowl.

The Decennial Census of Population in the United States is an example of an enumerative study. A process control chart is an example of an analytic study.

Dr. Deming shows that the relationship of the two physicians is important. If one is reliant on the other's good will, fear will cause him to agree with his senior in dependent inspection. Dr. Deming explains how the use of independent inspection helps the junior doctor to learn from differences that he has with the senior doctor.

From the theory of Profound Knowledge (see the system of Profound Knowledge on page 42), we know that there is no such thing as a true value. The agreement of the inspectors merely shows that a system of measurement exists.

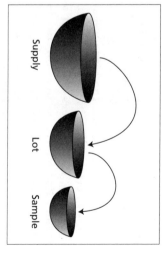

Many questionnaires use ratings. They are used to predict the future, and in that sense they are analytic. Even if one asks all the members of a class to rate the class, they constitute only a sample of all those that could have attended or will attend in the future. This is not even a random sample.

Analytic and Enumerative Studies—Why versus What (Continued)

TYPE	PURPOSE	EXAMPLE
Enumerative Study	To learn what conditions exist	The census will show the number of people who meet the definition of poverty
Analytic Study	To learn why conditions exist	Hands-on research will show why people are in poverty.

"How should the results be interpreted?" The answer is "with caution." Even a well-designed random sample only tells us what we would have gotten if we had applied the same questions to everyone in the list of sample members. Researchers call this list a frame. For many reasons, the list is often incomplete. It is the decision of the substantive expert whether the data of an incomplete list have value. Many surveys are flawed. In that situation, the interpretation of the data becomes even more subjective. In opinion surveys, respondents often give what they perceive to be the "socially correct" answer. At other times, respondents tell us what they think we want to hear. These factors exist, scales or not. There are many ways in which a survey can introduce bias. The total error of a survey depends on the sampling error and the bias. Both may be so large that the survey results are meaningless.

The results of a survey do not give any probability that a future action will give a stated result. However, a survey may give indications that a substantive expert could use.

It would be better to spend survey dollars by taking several small samples over time instead of spending it on one big sample. A series of readings gives a better feeling of what the Supply Bowl is like than does one big

sample. In effect, we can make a control chart of the survey data.

For display purposes, one could use Tukey's Box and Whisker plot. This graph will show the distribution and spread of the responses. Any good text, such as *Exploratory Data Analysis*, by John W. Tukey (Addison-Wesley 1977), explains how to form the chart.

We Only Did Our Best

As three o'clock approaches, I think back on all the new and important issues that we covered. Dr. Deming started with a theory; the system of Profound Knowledge. I learned a lot about systems. A system has to have an aim and it must be managed to be successful. I learned that I must do more than I did in the past. Understand variation, Dr. Deming said. I thought that I did, but it was not until the lesson of the beads that it came home to me what he meant.

I struggled with the theory of knowledge. New material kept coming with the pace of an express train. The concept of psychology was easier. I had learned some of this at school.

The 14 points, the deadly diseases, and the obstacles all were not exactly new but in this context were unknown to me. I see a lot of opportunity for improvement by understanding these ideas. It will take some time to digest all of the thoughts presented the last four days. With luck and working with one of the conference leaders, I hope to understand and start a transformation of myself first and my company next.

Some people had planes to catch. I was going to do the same but hated to miss any of the last words of wisdom from Dr. Deming. I changed my reservation and am glad that I did. What I heard this afternoon helped me to focus on what I need to do on my return to work.

Dr. Deming looks at his watch. "It is time to finish," he says. "I leave you with five little words." He counts the words on his fingers, **"We only did our best."**

For a moment the audience sits silently and then breaks out in spirited, standing applause. Dr. Deming, pleased, acknowledges the applause. As it dies down, he picks up his papers, says goodbye to his helpers, autographs one or two more books, and then leaves.

THE END

Epilogue

Dr. Deming's Four-Day Seminar was completed in the previous section. The material that follows is our view of what can be done to implement his philosophy.

Where Do We Go from Here

We have begun a journey. Some interesting ideas were generated by reading this book. How can these be implemented? How can the theories be put into practice? What to do next?

It depends on the situation of the reader. What is your current state? Where are you now? What is the state of the organization? What is your position within that organization? Each of these factors affects your personal road map for transformation.

The State of the Organization

Let's examine the various conditions and what actions you can take. Take, for instance, the state of the organization. We have identified four possible states:

1. Predisposed to Dr. Deming's system

These are companies and other organizations that have decided to undergo the transformation to managing under a system of Profound Knowledge.

2. Not predisposed to Dr. Deming's system because they never heard of it

These are organizations concerned with the quality of their products and services. They are unaware of the principles taught by Dr. Deming.

3. Not predisposed to Dr. Deming's system because they use another system to achieve quality

These are organizations that have adopted some form of management system to achieve quality. These systems may or may not parallel Dr. Deming's teaching. If they are, in fact, totally parallel, one is in the same position as in number 1 above. If there is divergence from the Deming philosophy, the greater the divergence, the more the Deming philosophy will be treated with distrust.

4. Not predisposed to Dr. Deming's system because they are apathetic to the issue of quality

Overview

The issue of quality was never raised before. Everyone is happy with the status quo. To suggest change is the equivalent of rocking the boat, not to be done.

If you are in the first two states, chances are good that you can accomplish something. If you are in the third state, which essentially encompasses the basic principles of Dr. Deming under some other name, things can get done as well.

If you are in the third state using a different method, it will take a massive marketing job to change people's positions. There are entrenched positions that can point to a large body of history. In this situation a failure of the system will convince the powers to be that a change is needed. The odds are good that such a failure will eventually occur.

Determine your organizational state

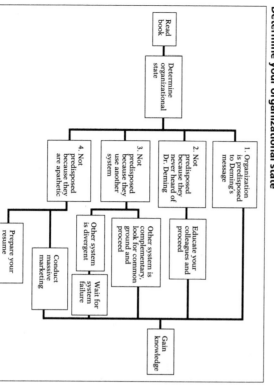

State 4 is easier to handle than state 3. It requires a marketing campaign to illustrate the benefits of the new management philosophy. Depending on the reader's position in the company, this state takes differing amounts of work.

At which state is your organization?

Level of Authority

A second consideration for the reader is the level of authority he or she possesses. Depending on the level of authority and the organizational state, several actions are possible.

Chief Executive Officer, Owner, or Principal

If you are a *CEO, owner, or principal (CEO henceforth)* of a firm, you can set the tone of the organization. That is not to say that you can dictate the management style. Such an abrupt change is likely to wreak havoc in the organization. Your strategy needs to be one of evolution rather than revolution. You want the changes you desire to be permanent and not be the change of the month. Slow evolution leads to permanent transformation.

To accomplish the evolution from a current state to a company transformed in the Deming philosophy, the CEO or equivalent needs help. Dr. Deming always talked about the need for a critical mass of managers to allow the transformation to happen. Until this number of managers is on board with the process, very little can be done. Once the critical mass has been reached, the process goes forward getting ever faster.

What constitutes a critical mass? Dr. Deming, at a meeting of masters, once said—we think jokingly—"a critical mass is the square root of the number of managers involved." It does not have to be a majority of the management team. It has be sufficiently large and wide spread that the 14 obligations can be adopted and implemented in a consistent manner throughout the organization.

The CEO in an organization that has adopted the Deming philosophy needs to guide his or her management team in a thorough understanding of the philosophy. Usually it is good to take the time to study the system of Profound Knowledge and the 14 obligations until the whole team understands it. Actually, it is not enough to understand it intellectually—it must become part of the make-up of management.

Whether through the use of a master to guide the process or through study groups described below, the CEO and the master, if there is one, leads the group in a discussion and dissection of Dr. Deming's teaching. It is recommended that the philosophical approach be labeled the "Name of Company Corporate philosophy" rather than the "Deming philosophy."

In going through the learning stage, the CEO or the master should make use of the questions appended to this section of the book. The questions need study and self-introspection to achieve their objective. Not all questions appear applicable. Nevertheless, it is good discipline and learning practice to answer all questions. Several approaches for using the questions are outlined below. The more work that is put into the process, the more benefit is gained.

As CEO, the use of alternative methods of managing for quality can be overcome fairly simply. For instance, the use of alternative

Determine Level of Authority

methods of achieving quality can be reviewed for benefit and compared to the Deming philosophy. With the CEO and a critical mass of managers asking for the Deming philosophy, it would be surprising if we did not get the response looked for by this group.

High-level Manager

If the reader is a high-level manager, such as a general manager of a division of a corporation, or a president or other officer of a firm, the reader can proceed in much the same way as the CEO. The only difference is that the high-level manager must also plan on selling the concept to the top executives and to his or her equals.

In proceeding to sell the philosophy of managing for quality, it is best if the executive first sells his or her peers. By getting affirmation from others at the same level, the executive ensures that not only is a critical mass supporting him or her but also a ready-made critical mass exists for the top management.

The basic technique for selling the peer group is to invite them to seminar sessions, led by the executive. In these sessions, the philosophy is thoroughly reviewed, taken apart, synthesized, and discussed. The assistance of a master is very valuable for this purpose. How such a person is found is discussed below.

Top executives are impressed by performance. The application of the Deming philosophy, whether under this name or under a corporate designation, often yields positive results quickly. When applied in the areas over which the executive has control, the positive aspects of the philosophy show up. This is often enough to convince top management in the efficacy of the philosophy.

Other Type of Reader

If you have *no budgetary authority* but you see a benefit to the company, your success depends a great deal upon the organizational state. One generalization we advise to all, "Go carefully. Don't lose your job."

In the case of State 1 (see page 196) the company is in accord with you. Your task in this situation is to join the system. Try to learn who is the champion, actual or designated. If there is no real champion apparent, an opportunity exists for you.

State 1 is an organization desiring to incorporate the Deming philosophy. This means that there is a person or a group interested in the process. Such a person or group has to be in authority in order for State 1 to exist. If there is no champion in such a set of circumstances, it will be useful for you to volunteer for this position. The person supporting the change becomes your sponsor and some of her or his authority passes on to you.

If there is a champion, work with this person. There are many areas where you can be of material assistance. It becomes an opportunity to be an authority.

In the case of an organization in State 2, there exists an opportunity to introduce a new concept. One has to be careful in how this is done. Approach this as a marketing challenge. Who is the decision maker that must be influenced? What is the decision maker's "hot button?" Is the decision maker cost oriented? Is the decision maker product oriented? Is the decision maker customer oriented? etc. By finding the best approach one can plan a campaign to influence the decision maker. In some cases, the decision is not made by an individual, but by a group of individuals.

Be prepared for your marketing plan to succeed. If it does, there is a strong possibility that you will be asked to implement the process. Be prepared for such an eventuality by preparing a plan in advance.

A more difficult case exists when the organization does not recognize the value of the Deming philosophy. Our caveat of retaining your job is useful here. A direct criticism of the organization's philosophy, no matter how justified, does not help. If anything, it draws the battle lines more firmly.

A possible approach is again to identify the decision maker and the key issues driving this person. Once more the approach is one of marketing. If the decision maker's mind is cast in concrete, no reasoning will help. In fact, the opposite can take place. In this type of situation, the best that you can do is to apply such items of the Deming philosophy as you can within your authority. As this philosophy helps to make you and your colleagues better employees, management will see the improvement, hopefully, leading to promotion. As the promotion gives you more scope of authority, use this to implement more and more of Dr. Deming's concepts.

The Need for a Master

What is a master? Dr. Deming often advised people to get a master to help them with actualizing the Deming philosophy in a company. What he meant by a master was a person who understood the system of Profound Knowledge and who could help a firm to apply this concept. A master then needs to be perfectly conversant with the theory of systems, with variation, with the philosophical underpinnings of knowledge, and with psychology. A master must also understand these concepts in relation to the 14 obligations, the seven deadly diseases, and the many obstacles to performance. The master's task is to help the client to understand these theoretical concepts and help the client to implement them.

Of the nearly thirty people recognized by Dr. Deming as a master, nineteen hold a doctorate. A large number of the masters studied under Dr. Deming. Academic degrees, by themselves, do not make a master in the sense used by Dr. Deming. What is important is the mastery of the system of Profound Knowledge.

How to Identify a Master

Anyone can claim to be a master. There is no registry of masters as such. How can one identify a master? Before his death, Dr. Deming established The W. Edwards Deming Institute in Washington, DC. This institute can refer you to masters. Also there are companies that have employed masters (Ford and GM, among others). These may be able to give a lead. These companies also employed many unqualified people. Another source of information is the Quality Enhancement Seminars, which use masters to give seminars about Dr. Deming's work. In addition, masters can refer you to other masters when they cannot undertake to help you themselves.

A master will assess your requirements for transformation. The master will take into consideration your organizational structure and can tell you how best to approach the task of training and implementation. He or she can help you in setting the proper pace for the transformation. The master will insist that things be done properly.

Every organization is different. A difference in people leads to different cultures. There is no single approach to the transformation. The approach depends on the cultural patterns of each organization.

Beware of supposed masters who have a canned solution to propose. Jim Bakken, formerly Vice President at Ford Motor Company, was quoted by Dr. Deming as saying that what people want is instant pudding. Open can; add water; stir and you have instant quality.

What can you do if no master is available? Is it still possible to profit from this book and the questions in this chapter? The answer is "yes." One uses a method of experiential learning.

Experiential Learning

Experiential learning derives its name from the concept that adults have a great deal of life experience. If they bring this experience to a group session of other adults to work on a specific question, sharing individual experiences helps not only to resolve the question but also to have all members of the group gain insights not otherwise possible.

Dr. Deming clearly warns that executives sharing experience without theory learn nothing and may even do harm. This learning method requires that a theory be formed first from the questions. Then experiential learning discussing the theory can help. The authors recommend obtaining a master. Only in the absence of a master should one resort to this method. It has inherent dangers.

At the end of this section are a number of questions. These were adapted from the questions Dr. Deming used in his Four-Day Seminar. They have been directed toward members of a single organization forming the group of learners.

In the absence of a master, form a group of five or six people interested in coming together to study the questions at the end of this chapter. In order to study under the best conditions, set a regular meeting day and time. Keep to this schedule as much as possible. Deviations tend to lessen the impact of the study as well as give the impression of a lack of importance.

Every member of the team is given an assignment. The assignments are rotated each meeting. The following are the assignments and their job description:

- **Reader.** The reader reads the question that the group works on. He or she repeats this to the group as often as needed.
- **Reporter.** The reporter records the group's answers on a work sheet to file in a log book available for reference later on.
- **Encourager.** The encourager encourages full participation by asking all members to offer their opinions, views, or answers. The encourager keeps track of the time as decided by the team.

Transformation Process

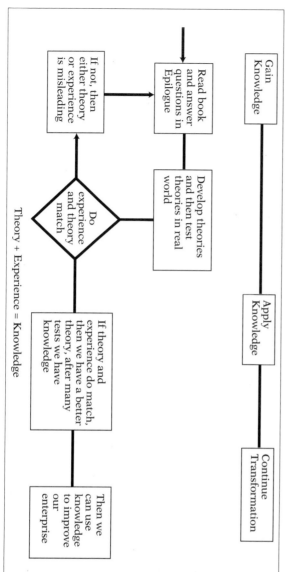

Gain Knowledge → Apply Knowledge → Continue Transformation

Read book and answer questions in Epilogue

Develop theories and then test theories in real world

Do experience and theory match

If not, then either theory or experience is misleading

If theory and experience do match, then we have a better theory, after many tests we have knowledge

Then we can use knowledge to improve our enterprise

Theory + Experience = Knowledge

- **Calculator.** The calculator does the calculations that may be required. The checker checks these calculations.
- **Devil's Advocate.** This is the person in the group who challenges the group's response to the question. This is a very important function. If the group can justify their position in spite of keen questioning, the response is probably robust and likely to be correct. If the group is shaken by the devil's advocate, it is an indication that their response was not as well thought out as it should have been. As Mr. Scherkenbach pointed out, both the group and the devil's advocate must have theory.
- **Checker.** The checker has two responsibilities. First, he or she checks every individual response for correctness as needed. Second, the checker checks every answer if the group submits a group response. The checker is also responsible for making sure everyone knows and can explain the answers.

Study each question carefully. If need be, refer back to the text. If at all possible, have your responses reviewed by a master with commentary. If no master is available for this, have the material reviewed by a knowledgeable peer. Review the feedback and learn by comparing it to your theory of the issue.

Deming User Groups

Deming user groups (DUGs) are another way for the reader to study with other interested parties. For a list of these groups contact Quality Enhancement Seminars in Los Angeles, California. User groups differ in character: Some have speakers on general topics related to the Deming philosophy. These can be a good source of networking for the reader. If the speaker has time, questions can be asked. Be careful, not every speaker is a master.

Some groups employ a master to lead them through a series of learning steps. These groups have the advantage of having advanced knowledge. A few groups have exercises for the members. When performed under the tutelage of a master, these can be very powerful. If a hack holds these exercises, they may be bad to harmful. DUG's are a good source of peers for reviewing the question answers.

Deming Scholars Intern Program (Fordham University)

Fordham University has a Deming Scholars program. This program is an 18-month full-time program of study and internships. It is taught and supervised by masters. This is the best way for a beginner or intermediate student to learn about the Deming philosophy.

The Deming Scholars spend six weeks in internships between classes. Companies that sponsor a scholar get the benefit of someone who has been thoroughly trained in the Deming philosophy. Study groups could take advantage of the scholars' internships.

How to Do Self-study

If you are totally dependent upon yourself, there are no study groups within reach, and no Deming user groups are available, then you must rely on your readings. These, supplemented by long answers to the questions, form the framework of your studies. If at all possible, it is helpful to work with a study partner. Any sympathetic soul with the desire to learn about the philosophy will do. Beware, however, that it easy for two partners to slip into major errors simply because neither has the knowledge required to get the proper answer.

Colleges and Universities

To our knowledge, at this time the only program supervised by a committee of masters is at Fordham Graduate School of Business. It is likely that a number of schools will have programs in the future that match the quality of Fordham's offering. We hope that many more good institutions will undertake this type of work.

Questions for Discussion

Day 1—The Need for Transformation of Western Management

1. What, in your judgment, might be the basic cause of the deficit of the United States in manufactured goods?

2. a. What changes have taken place over the world in the last three decades that affect North America?

   b. Is change in style of management required?

   c. Explain why it is that solving problems, stamping out fires, patch work, and cosmetic changes are not the transformation that Dr. Deming says must take place in North America?

3. Explain some of the sources of heaviest loss from the prevailing style of management. Explain why these losses can not be measured, yet why these losses must be managed.

4. Explain why it is wrong to suppose that if you cannot measure something, you cannot manage it.

A System of Profound Knowledge

Concept of System

5. Why does Dr. Deming propose a system of Profound Knowledge?

6. What does he mean by a system?

7. Why must there be an aim for a system?

8. Explain why it is that the components of a system cannot, by themselves, state the aim of the system nor accomplish it—the system must be managed.

9. Whose job is it to clarify the aim of the system?

10. What does Dr. Deming mean by "optimization of a system?"

11. a. Explain (if you agree) that optimization by which everybody may gain requires re-orientation of the prevailing systems of management in industry, education, and government.

    b. What changes are required?

12. Give examples of low interdependence between components of a system, and examples of high interdependence.

13. a. Show that for the optimization of a system, some divisions in the company may voluntarily operate below maximum profit, or even at a loss, yet everybody may prosper at a maximum, including the division that, for optimization of the whole company, operated at a loss.

    b. Why is it that the performance (e.g., sales, profit) of any component such as an individual, team, or division ought for optimization to be appraised in terms of its contribution to the whole organization, not for its own profit?

14. a. Explain why everybody loses from failure to optimize the system.

    b. Give two examples of losses from failure to optimize the system.

15. Why is precise optimization not necessary? (To answer this, explain the loss function and its contact with minimum loss.)

16. Will enlargement of a committee necessarily improve results?

17. Can you substantiate Dr. Deming's statement that Profound Knowledge must come from the outside? Or do you have other thoughts?

18. Is it good for people to get together for exchange of ideas? Will they generate Profound Knowledge?

Theory of Knowledge

19. Why is it that planning requires prediction? (Give some simple examples.)

19. a. What do you mean by a rational plan?
    b. Explain why any rational plan involves prediction.

20. Is substantive (subject matter) knowledge necessary for useful prediction? Why?

21. Does a large number of examples establish a theory? Why?

22. Does a single unexplained failure require abandonment or modification of a theory? (Yes.)

23. May one construct a theory based on one example? Which comes first, the theory or the example? (Answer: the theory.)

24. Can degree of belief in a prediction be quantified as .8, .9, .99?

25. Why is it that experience by itself teaches nothing?

26. Explain why possession of theory helps one to ask meaningful questions.

27. What is a requirement for knowledge—i.e., when does a statement convey knowledge? (Answer. When it predicts, and fits past events.)

28. Explain why interpretation of the results of a test or experiment is prediction.

Understanding Psychology

29. Why is some knowledge of psychology a good idea for a manager or maybe for anybody?

30. Where has innovation of product come from, as a matter of history: from the customer or from the producer?

31. a. What is a requisite for innovation?
    b. What forces smother innovation?
    c. What forces build up extrinsic motivation?

32. What may be the result of overjustification? Does your company furnish examples?

33. a. Explain why best efforts can do more harm than good.
    b. Explain that we need best efforts to be guided by theory.

34. What are some of the changes that Dr. Deming says must be made in the prevailing style of management?

35. What might be the effect of these changes? (Answer: joy in work, joy in learning, cooperation.)

Understanding Variation

36. What is the job of a manager of people? Would ranking them help them?

37. What are the sources of power of a manager of people?

38. What is the effect of the prevailing style of reward? (Ranking children, people, teams, divisions, and companies with reward at the top and punishment at the bottom accentuates the evils of ranking.)

39. a. Explain that if ten people, teams, divisions, costs, etc., are compared, one of them will be highest, and one of them will be lowest. Why is it necessary to understand something about the theory of variation in order to predict anything about differences in the future?
    b. Explain that one or more will be below average, no matter whether they all are superb or all in disgrace. Explain that it is necessary to solve problems and to stamp out fires that break out.

Obligation 1

40. How does a statement of constancy of purpose help people in the company to understand what their jobs are?

41. How does a flow diagram help people to understand what their jobs are?

42. How are the following people served by a statement of constancy of purpose?

- Employees
  - Hourly
  - Salaried
- Management
- The community
- The country
- Customers
- Suppliers
- Stockholders

43. Why is it good for anyone to have a theory for accomplishment of an aim?

44. What might be the effect if the management were to issue a statement of constancy of purpose and not provide a climate for fulfillment? Would some faulty management practices (such as MBO, merit system, incentive pay) nullify a statement of constancy of purpose?

45. Can Obligation 1 be separated from the remaining 13 Obligations? Can any of the obligations be separated from the others? What is the aim and the theory behind the 14 Obligations?

Obligation 2

46. How could you help top management to learn the new philosophy? How could you help them to put it into practice?

47. a. What may a satisfied customer do? (Switch.) What kind of customer do we need? Where is the source of greatest profit?

   b. Is it sufficient for the future to have satisfied customers today?

   c. What business are we in? Explain why this is a good question to keep in mind.

Obligation 3

48. Explain why we shall almost always need inspection of product and of service.

49. a. Can you name some examples where 100 percent inspection is more economical than no inspection? (Page 50 will help on this question.)

   b. What might you mean by 100 percent inspection?

   c. Describe examples in which 100 percent inspection is mere dilution of responsibility. Explain the dangers of diluted responsibility.

50. What comments do you have in respect to audit of compliance?

51. If two or more inspectors work on the same stream of product, under what conditions may we compare their results to learn whether we have a system of inspection? (See page 177 of the text.)

Obligation 4

52. Under what conditions would price tag be a good basis for award of business? Are these conditions ever met in the world of experience?

53. What should be the aims of customer and supplier? Explain how cooperation brings greater profit to both.

54. Contrast long-term relationship of loyalty and trust with the traditional practice of doing business on price tag with short-term contracts. (Long-term relationship implies continual joint effort to improve quality and to decrease costs.)

55. a. Explain that uniformity should be one of the aims in continuing purchase of materials and service.

   b. Might a long-term contract with a sole supplier increase the number of options for cooperation between customer and supplier?

56. What are some of the advantages of having a single supplier for any one item of product or service?
   - Incoming manufactured material or subassembly
   - Manufactured product
   - Service
   - A commodity

57. What about batteries and standby generating equipment to throw into duty in the event of failure of the main source of electricity? Is this an example of a second supplier for a service?

58. a. Are the obligations of customer and supplier to each other intensified if the supplier is the sole supplier for an item?
   b. Is investment on the part of the supplier more attractive under a long-term contract?

59. a. What in your judgment are some important criteria for choice of single supplier?
   b. Why might you not be hasty in your choice?

60. a. Are there some risks in having a sole supplier for an item?
   b. Would two suppliers eliminate these risks or multiply them?

61. A pamphlet on the obligations of a supplier contained this statement:
   The supplier is responsible for the quality of his product.
   a. What is wrong with this statement?
   b. Can either one alone, supplier or customer, be the sole judge?
   c. Would this statement build a fruitful relationship between supplier and customer?
   d. Does the customer always know what he needs? (No. Under good relationship between customer and supplier, they will work together to arrive at the most economical satisfaction of the needs of the customer.)

62. After a considerable amount of worry, the vice-president of manufacturing concludes that costs for a certain subassembly are too high. He asks the purchasing department to get new bids on all parts that go into the subassembly. What effects might this have on the cost and quality of the final product?

63. A customer sent out the following notice to all suppliers:
   We expect a 1 percent decrease in cost every year for five years.
   What might well be the effect of such a notice? Would suppliers try to meet the demand? How? What might happen to their quality? Will this demand build a good relationship between customer and supplier? Does this demand absolve the customer from responsibility?

Obligation 5

64. What are four requirements for improvement of quality?

65. Have you observed some improvement during the past two years in the product and service that you purchase? Some deterioration?

66. What about your own work? How have you improved in your work? In your relationship with other people?

67. Why may better uniformity of output decrease costs? What about better uniformity in time of delivery?

68. If your company had a monopoly or unassailable position in some product or service, what would you say about the obligation of your company to improve product, quality, and productivity?

69. A plant closed. Did it close because of poor workmanship in the plant? Why did it close?

70. A bank closed. Did it close because of sluggishness and mistakes of tellers? Because of mistakes in bank statements? Mistakes in calculation of interest due? Why did it close?

71. Why have many attempts at OC-Circles, Employee Involvement, and Quality of Work Life fizzled out after a few months? What are some conditions for success of such activities?

Obligation 6

72. State some important principles in learning and in teaching a skill. Why is it necessary to provide training in different ways?

Obligation 7

73. Explain why it is that about half of any group will be below average, no matter how figures on performance be obtained, whether the figures make sense or not.

74. A well-regarded supervisor held out for examination and discussion the defective items that her seven people made during the day. She would spend the last half-hour of the day with her seven people for examination and scrutiny of every defective item produced that day. The system of production of defective items was stable.

a. Explain the principle by which the supervisor here, with the best of intentions and best efforts, only made matters worse by showing her people the mistakes that they made today.

b. Under what conditions would it be good to show people their mistakes?

Obligation 8

75. a. Give some examples of fear and of anxiety.
b. Try to distinguish between fear and anxiety.

76. a. What are some sources of fear and mistrust?
b. How do fear and mistrust affect performance?

77. a. Name some possible causes of excessive anxiety.
b. How does excessive anxiety affect performance?

78. Anxiety about job security seems to be on the minds of many people, management, and hourly workers.

78. a. Take, for example, some plant that closed. Did it close because of laxness on the part of the people that worked there?

b. Will punctuality, hard work, and best efforts guarantee job security?

c. What must management do to enhance job security?

Obligation 9

79. Describe a systematic way in which three staff areas may, by cooperation, optimize their own profits. Would each staff area choose to maximize its own profit on every option? (No.)

80. How many options in total do you suppose the 200 companies mentioned by Dr. Ouchi on page 82 of the text considered? (Hundreds.)

81. Write down some examples of cooperation (win, win; no loser):

a. Between people
b. Between divisions or functions within a company
c. Between companies
d. Between countries
e. Between a government agency and industry

Day Two—The Lesson of the Beads

82. What information would it have been good for the management to have in hand before they set a price on white beads?

83. Why was it futile to set three beads as a price on white beads? What was wrong with the merit system that rewarded the worker with the fewest red beads any day? Why was it wrong to put on probation the worker with the greatest number of red beads any day?

84. Would it have been good if the management had worked with the supplier of beads to try to improve his process and thus to reduce the proportion of red beads in the incoming material?

85. What was wrong with the management's decision to keep the place open with the best workers? What is the meaning of best workers? Best when? Over what period?

86. Explain that management is not playing games; management is prediction. What rational basis was there for prediction that the best workers in the past would be best in the future? (None.)

87. How might the Willing Workers have improved their output of white beads had they been granted the privilege to try out suggestions on improvement of procedures?

88. What did the control limits tell us?

89. What are some of the advantages of a system that is stable enough to use for prediction? (The control limits for a stable system, if extended into the future, provide prediction of variation in the number of red beads in a workload, of the average, and of output.)

90. Suppose that you decided to repeat the experiment on the red beads under the same conditions. What would you mean by the "same conditions?"
Same paddle? Yes. See data on different paddles.
Same beads? Yes. The results with different beads—same number red and white—could be very different.
Same procedures? Yes. How could you ensure continuance of the same procedures?

91. What barriers (red beads) may there be to pride of workmanship in your own job?

92. Suppose that this company, working with the supplier of beads, was so successful that the average number of red beads per workload was 5 (instead of somewhere between 9 and 10). What would be the new control limits, and hence the variation to expect in the near future? (Answer: 11.4 for the upper limit and 0 for the lower limit.) The arithmetic gives 5 + 6.4 for the control limits. We use 0 for the lower limit because a negative number of red beads is meaningless.

Obligation 10

93. What is wrong with posters and slogans that ask workers in the plant to take pride in their work?

94. What about the poster, "Do it right the first time?"

95. What type of message on posters might be good?

Obligation 11

96. What happens when a work standard (time standard, quota) is replaced by competent leadership? (Productivity and quality go up.)

97. The president of a company asks for a report and resolution of every failure to meet a figure, every time one week falls short in some way of the week before, production in one hour falls short of the quota. What is wrong with this kind of management (management by results, or tampering, making things worse)?

98. Explain that a company and an individual must have aims, vision, challenge, and anxiety in some reasonable amount.

99. Describe the Shewhart Cycle of Learning, a flowchart for learning or for improvement: the PDSA Cycle.

Obligation 12

100. What are some of the handicaps that affect your own work?

101. Which of these handicaps may be of your own making?

102. Which handicaps can be corrected locally? Which handicaps require action by management?

103. How might management learn about these handicaps?

Obligation 13

104. In what ways might a company help and encourage employees to continue their education?

Obligation 14

105. Who is responsible for the transformation of an organization? How can everybody help? (Some suggestions are on pages 114 and 115 of the text.) Could you add some thoughts?

Day 3—Some Other Faulty Practices

106. What is wrong with incentive pay, and with alleged pay for performance (in number, dollars)? What is the result?

106. a. Emphasis on numbers? Dollars sold?

b. What may be the results when salesmen are paid for performance? What may happen if they are offered a bonus for reaching or exceeding a target by the end of June? Suggestions:

Offers to a customer an unauthorized discount. What is the result?

Promises immediate delivery even though the company cannot do this.

Sells to a customer more than he (customer) needs. Who loses? Who wins?

Salesman of life insurance sells more insurance than the customer can handle. Customer drops the policy; can't pay the premium. Who loses? Who wins?

A salesman for a copying machine sells to a customer a fancier machine than the customer needs. Who loses? Who wins?

Explain the effect of an urgent appeal to salesmen to make new records during the last month of the fiscal year. (Suggestion: management thinks that business is spurting; prepares for increase in business, only to suffer later the costs of overexpansion.)

107. What may be the losses from an overenthusiastic forecast?

108. a. Explain MBO as practiced.

b. Give two examples of MBO as practiced.

c. What was the effect of the use of MBO for each example above?

109. What is the effect of a daily or weekly quota?

a. What does MBO emphasize? (Numbers.)

b. Explain why it is that a quota demolishes any possibility to learn whether the system is stable.

c. Hence, a quota demolishes any chance to improve the system and to achieve greater output and better quality. Explain this.

d. What would happen if a plant manager ever reported production above his or her quota for the day?

e. What would happen if an individual worker ever reported production above his or her quota for the day?

110. A business plan consists of a matrix of targets, perhaps by quarter. Explain why it is that quarterly reports on the plan demolish any chance to improve the system (i.e., to decrease costs, or to shorten the time between states of development and production). Is this a form of MBO?

The Funnel and Tampering

111. Write down on the cards provided some examples of Rules 2, 3 and 4 of the funnel (tampering) that you have observed in your own company; in other companies; in government; in education; anywhere else. It is permissible to include examples described by Dr. Deming, but it would be good to add 10 more. (It is not important to remember by number the four rules for tampering that Dr. Deming described).

112. Do we like faults, defects, late deliveries, mistakes, accidents? Of course not, but what do we accomplish by action on a stable process on appearance of a fault, defect, red bead? (See pages 148 and 155.)
113. How would you describe tampering?
114. Can you measure the loss from tampering? (No.) Ought we manage it? (Yes.)

Operational Definitions

115. What is an operational definition?
116. Why are operational definitions desirable for business?
117. Read the following specifications. Which ones satisfy the criteria for an operational definition? (Hint: none. Please state why.)

Product	Specifications
HSLA Sheet Steel	No scratches
Pinion gear bar stock	Homogenous microstructure Blocky ferrite and pearlite
Axle tube OD	Must be round
Output shaft surface hardness	Rc 55 to Rc 57
Springs	Must be clean
Resistors	150 Kí 2 Watt
Bearing journal surface	Average roughness 8 to 15, peak count 80 to 100

118. Consider these as objectives:
Imperceptible shift
Improved fuel economy
Best-in-class transmission
Improved personal productivity

Day 4—Questions on Later Chapters

119. What may be wrong with automatic compensation to hold pieces within specifications to achieve zero defects? (page 137).

120. Describe the two mistakes that people may make in response to a fault, complaint, accident, or mistake (page 99). Do they both cause loss?
121. Why not reduce both of them to zero frequency of occurrence?
122. What did Dr. Shewhart propose?
123. Under what conditions does a process have a capability?
124. Suppose that someone says this: We are meeting specifications. We don't need to worry about statistical control of the process. Why is this risky?
125. May a process be in statistical control (stable, predictable) yet turn out, dependably, a predictable fraction of defective items (faults, mistakes)? (Yes.) Is the cost of these faults predictable? (Yes.) What should we try to do? When should we screen the output? (See page 50 and 51 and following.)
126. What is wrong with use of specification limits as control limits? (Tampering makes things worse.)
127. Could anyone compute the loss caused by this mistake?
128. Why does Just In Time require statistical control of processes?
129. Suppose that the difference between (a) repeated measurement taken on an instrument intended for use, and (b) a measurement taken on the standard, are "statistically significantly different." Is statistical significance a basis for adjustment? Why or why not? What principle ought to govern the decision on whether to adjust the instrument intended for use?
130. Why is it desirable that the use of instruments and gauges should show statistical control?
131. The chief accountant of a division asks for an explanation of any cost that departs more than 10 percent from the budget. What is wrong with this practice? Will this practice decrease or help to understand the causes of costs, and to decrease costs in the future? (No.)

132. Describe some run charts or control charts that may be helpful to management. The list may of course be varied and extended. Points may be plotted weekly or monthly.

Suggestions:

Accounts receivable, cause of delay in
    payment
Alleged wrong count
Alleged poor quality
Shipped to wrong address
Invoice fails to show discount promised
    by salesman
Goods arrived too late
Absences
Accidents, number, time lost
Proportion of orders shipped on time
Poor quality of some important product
    or service, in and out
Number of new customers
Number of failures in the premises to
    indicate presence of hazardous material or danger

133. Which charts (these or others) have you found to be most useful? Which ones showed a stable system?

134. Explain why the action to be taken is different when a chart shows a stable state from the action to be taken when the chart shows an unstable state.

Appendix

Some Notes on Statistical Process Control

In his four-day seminar, Dr. Deming always carried out the bead experiment on the second day. After completion of the data gathering, he created a control chart of the data on the overhead. Using the cover of the bead box as a straight edge, he drew the axis of the chart. Then he plotted the points. Finally, he computed the control limits. Using his own notation, he called the average beads per paddle, X-bar. He then computed the upper and lower control limits showing the formula to use.

To many in the audience, this was the first time they saw a control chart computed, constructed and used. It was easy. Some, who brought their own data, tried constructing a control chart using their data.

As facilitators, we often experienced people from the audience coming to us and saying that they tried using Dr. Deming's formula with their own data but it did not work. We quickly noted that their data was not applicable to the type of control chart used by Dr. Deming. He never mentioned that there are different types of charts for different types of data. These charts all have the same appearance and interpretation, but one computes them differently.

With this experience in mind, the authors suggest that those interested in this important tool continue with a separate study on the subject of control charts. Most courses on statistical process control will cover the most commonly used types of control charts, listed below:

For Variable Data

X-bar, R-Chart (Charts for Average and Range)
X-bar, s-Chart (Charts for Averages and Standard Deviation)

X, MR-Chart (Charts for individuals and Moving Range)

For Attribute Data

np-Chart (Chart for number of nonconforming items)
p-Chart (Chart for percentage of nonconforming items)
c-Chart (Chart for number of nonconformities)
u-Chart (Chart for ratio of nonconformities)

There are other less common charts. A thorough knowledge of the above charts will suffice for managing operations.

Statistical process control includes analysis of processes to make improvements. Dr. Juran and Dr. Ishikawa contributed such additional tools as the Cause-and-Effect Diagram (also called the Fishbone or Ishikawa diagram), Pareto Chart, Check Sheet, Run Chart, Histogram, and Correlation Charts.

While schools and organizations have short formal courses, the topic is sufficiently simple that self-study is possible. Many good books are available on these tools. We list here some books we know. The list is in order of simplicity as we see it.

AIAG (Automotive Industry Action Group), *Fundamental Statistical Process Control, Reference Manual, 1991.* Obtainable from AIAG Headquarters, Suite 200, 26200 Lahser Road, Southfield, MI 48034; telephone 313-358-3570. This is the simplest, best explanation of the mechanics of constructing and using control charts. Originally a Ford Motor Company publication, it remains largely unchanged. There is some new material on tampering.

Hy Pitt, *SPC for the Rest of Us*, Addison-Wesley Publishing Company, One Jacob Way, Reading, MA 01867. This book includes all seven tools.

213

American Society for Testing and Materials (ASTM), *Manual on Presentation of Data and Control Chart Analysis (STP 15D)* 1976. Available from the ASTM, 1916 Race Street, Philadelphia, PA 19103. This is a classic manual. Nearly all the great contributers to the field of quality control—Bicking, Deming, Dodge, Passano, Romig, Shewhart, Simon, etc.—were at one time or another members of the E-11 committee responsible for this publication. The first edition was issued in 1933!

Western Electric Co., Inc (AT&T Technologies), *Statistical Quality Control Handbook*, 1956. Available from AT&T Technologies, Commercial Sales Clerk, Select Code 700-444, P.O. Box 19901, Indianapolis, IN 46219; telephone 1-800-432-6600. This work, completed under the chairmanship of Bonnie Small, is still an excellent source of information concerning control charts.

Wheeler, D. J. and D. S. Chambers, *Understanding Statistical Process Control*, Second Edition, 1992. Obtainable from SPC Press Inc., 5908 Toole Drive, Knoxville, TN 37919, telephone: 615-584-5005. This is a fine text on the topic. The text covers more than the mechanics of Statistical Quality Control, it covers much of the theory to aid the user in applying the correct theory.

The Funnel Rules Applied to the Red Bead Experiment

Dr. Michael D. Tveite showed Dr. Deming that the result of the lesson of the red beads can be applied to the various rules of the funnel. To keep the numbers from becoming too large, he subtracted a constant from each number. A good choice for this constant is the nearest whole number of the average number of red beads. In the lesson of the red beads, the average number of red beads per drawing was 9.1. In the example illustrated at the right, a 9 was subtracted from each number of red beads in column 2 and posted as d_1 in column 4.

Dr. Tveite plotted the results. From the plot, the effect of tampering can be seen dramatically.

Since some of the participants at the seminar had a problem getting Dr. Tveite's plots, Mr. Latzko prepared the table on the next page and the instructions shown below.

Instruction for the Funnel Movement Table (Where F_i = the funnel position under rule i and d_i = position of marble under rule i)

1. Post the number of red beads from Day Two exercise in sequence of production. This is shown in the second column of the table on page 216.

2. Subtract Target (T) value from number of red beads in column 2. Post the result in column 4 (labeled d_1). Do this for every one of the 24 rows. Remember that the subtraction is algebraic. For example, if the count of red beads is 8 and the target is 10, the answer is 8 − 10 = −2. The sign of the answer is important.

3. For Rule 2, compute d_2 by algebraically adding d_1 to F_2. The formula is

$d_2 = F_2 + d_1$.
For example, if $F_2 = -3$ and
$d_1 = -1$, then $d_2 = (-3) + (-1) = -4$.

4. For Rule 2, compute the funnel movement as follows: F_2 for the new row is F_2 of the previous row minus d_2. New $F_2 =$ Old $F_2 − d_2$. For example, if the old F_2 is −3 and d_2 is −4, then the next row's F_2 is

New $F_2 = (-3) - (-4) = +1$
since the term − (−4) equals +4 and
(−3) + 4 = +1.

5. For Rule 3, compute d_3 by algebraically adding d_1 to F_3. The formula is $d_3 = F_3 + d_1$.
For example, if $F_3 = 0$ and $d_1 = 2$, then
$d_3 = 0 + 2 = +2$.

6. For Rule 3, compute the funnel movement as follows: F_3 for the new row is 0 minus d_3. New $F_3 = 0 - d_3$. For example, if d_3 is –4, then the next row's F_3 is New $F_3 = 0 - (-4) = +4$.

7. For Rule 4, compute d_3 by algebraically adding d_1 to F_4. The formula is $d_4 = F_4 + d_1$.

   For example, if $F_4 = 5$ and $d_1 = -1$, then $d_4 = 5 + (-1) = +4$.

8. For Rule 4, compute the funnel movement as follows: F_4 for the new row is d_4. New $F_4 =$ Old d_4. For example, if the old d_4 is –4, then the next row's F_4 is New $F_4 = (-4) = -4$.

The Funnel Rules Applied to the Red Bead Experiment

Seq. #	Red Beads	Rule 1		Rule 2		Rule 3		Rule 4	
		F_1	d_1	F_2	d_2	F_3	d_3	F_4	d_4
1	9	0	0	0	0	0	0	0	0
2	7	0	-2	0	-2	0	-2	0	-2
3	12	0	3	2	5	2	5	-2	1
4	7	0	-2	-3	-5	-5	-7	1	-1
5	8	0	-1	2	1	7	6	-1	-2
6	9	0	0	1	1	-6	-6	-2	-2
7	8	0	-1	0	-1	6	5	-2	-3
8	8	0	-1	1	0	-5	-6	-3	-4
9	12	0	3	1	4	6	9	-4	-1
10	8	0	-1	-3	-4	-9	-10	-1	-2
11	7	0	-2	1	-1	10	8	-2	-4
12	10	0	1	2	3	-8	-7	-4	-3
13	16	0	7	-1	6	7	14	-3	4
14	14	0	5	-7	-2	-14	-9	4	9
15	7	0	-2	-5	-7	9	7	9	7
16	13	0	4	2	6	-7	-3	7	11
17	5	0	-4	-4	-8	3	-1	11	7
18	6	0	-3	4	1	1	-2	7	4
19	6	0	-3	3	0	2	-1	4	1
20	12	0	3	3	6	1	4	1	4
21	5	0	-4	-3	-7	-4	-8	4	0
22	10	0	1	4	5	8	9	0	1
23	13	0	4	-1	3	-9	-5	1	5
24	6	0	-3	-4	-7	5	2	5	2

The Four Funnel Rules Applied to the Red Beads

Funnel Rule 1

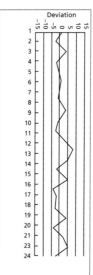

Rule 1: Don't move funnel

- Random pattern
- Common causes of variation only
- Lowest total variation

Example:
Do not adjust system unnecessarily.

Funnel Rule 2

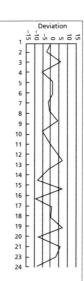

Rule 2: Move funnel in equal and opposite direction of marble from last position of funnel

- Random pattern
- Common causes of variation
- Double the variance of Rule 1

Example:
Adjust in equal opposite direction from target value.
Automatic machine adjustment based on measurement.
Note: Chart 2 points are wider than Chart 1.

Funnel Rule 3

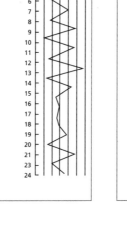

Rule 3: Move funnel in equal and opposite direction of marble from funnel rest position

- Nonrandom pattern; alternating cycles
- Special causes of variation
- Ever-expanding variation

Example:
"Use it or lose it" budget policy.

Funnel Rule 4

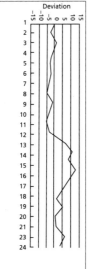

Rule 4: Move funnel over last position of marble.

- Nonrandom pattern. Goes to infinity in one direction.
- Special causes of variation
- Ever-expanding variation

Example:
Worker training worker.

Bibliography

American Society for Testing and Materials, *Moisture Content Determination: Oven Drying Method D 644.*

_____, Committee E-11 on Statistical Methods. *ASTM Manual on Presentation of Data and Control Chart Analysis,* fourth revision. Philadelphia, PA: ASTM Special Technical Publication 15D, 1976.

Automotive Industry Action Group, (AIAG), *Fundamental Statistical Process Control,* Southfield, MI: AIAG, 1991.

AT&T Technologies: Bonnie Small, editor, *Statistical Quality Control Handbook,* Indianapolis, IN: Western Electric Co., Inc., 1956.

Bly, Robert, *Iron John,* Reading, MA: Addison-Wesley, 1990.

Bross, Irving, *Design for Decision,* New York: Macmillan, 1953.

Creveling, C. M. and William Fowlkes, *Engineering Methods for Robust Design: Advanced Taguchi Methods,* Reading, MA: Addison-Wesley, 1995.

Deming, W. E., *Elementary Principles of the Statistical Control of Quality,* Second Printing, June 1952. Tokyo: Nippon Kagaku Gijutsu Remmei, 1951.

_____, *Some Theory of Sampling,* New York: John Wiley & Sons, 1950. Reprint Dover 1984.

_____, *Quality, Productivity and Competitive Position,* Cambridge, MA: Massachusetts Institute of Technology, Center for Advanced Engineering Study, 1982.

_____, *Out of the Crisis,* Cambridge, MA: Massachusetts Institute of Technology, Center for Advanced Engineering Study, 1986.

_____, *Foundation for Management of Quality in the Western World,* paper delivered at a meeting of the Institute of Management Science in Osaka, 24 July 1989, updated 1 September 1990.

_____, *The New Economics,* Cambridge, MA: Massachusetts Institute of Technology, Center for Advanced Engineering Study, 1993.

Deming, W. E. and L. Geoffry, "On Sample Inspection in the Processing of Census," *Journal of the American Statistical Association* Vol. 36, September 1941.

Early, Pete, *Family of Spies,* New York: Bantam Books, 1988.

Ishikawa, Kaoru, *Guide to Quality Control,* 2nd Revised Edition, Tokyo: Asian Productivity Organization, 1986.

Joiner, Brian L., *Fourth Generation Management: The New Business Consciousness,* Madison, WI: Joiner Associates, 1994.

Kapsales, Peter, *The Age of Punishment.* Unpublished manuscript, May 1991.

Killian, Cecelia S., *The World of W. Edwards Deming,* Second Edition, Knoxville, TN: SPC Press, 1992.

Latzko, William J., "Reduction of Mistakes in a Bank," in W. Edwards Deming, *Quality, Productivity, and Competitive Position.* Cambridge, MA: Massachusetts Institute of Technology, Center for Advanced Engineering Study, 1982.

———, *Quality and Productivity for Bankers and Financial Managers,* New York: Marcel Dekker, 1987.

———, "Control Charts in the Board Room" in *The Forty-Third Annual Quality Congress Proceedings,* Toronto, American Society for Quality Control, 1989.

Latzko, William J. and J. D. Dowhin, "Achieving Service Quality by Charting," in *The Forty-Fifth Annual Quality Congress Proceedings.* Milwaukee, WI: American Society for Quality Control, 1991.

Mann, Nancy R., *The Keys to Excellence,* Third Edition, Los Angeles: Prestwick Books, 1989.

Moen, Ronald D., Thomas W. Nolan, and Lloyd P. Provost, *Improving Quality Through Planned Experimentation,* New York: McGraw-Hill, 1991.

Neave, Henry R., *The Deming Dimension,* Knoxville, TN: SPC Press, 1990.

Orsini, Joyce, "Bonuses: What is the Impact?" *National Productivity Review,* Spring 1987.

Ouchi, William G., *The M-Form Society,* Reading, MA: Addison-Wesley, 1984.

Peck, Scott, *The Road Less Traveled: A New Psychology of Love, Traditional Values, and Spiritual Growth,* New York: Simon and Schuster, 1978.

Phadke, Madhav S., *Quality Engineering Using Robust Design,* Englewood Cliffs, NJ: Prentice Hall, 1989.

Pitt, Hy, *SPC for the Rest of Us,* Reading, MA: Addison-Wesley, 1994.

Saunders, David, Mark Cary, Bonnie Kay, Paul Orleman, Wayne Robertshaw, Gabriel Ross, Wallace Wallace, and John Wittenbraker, "The Customer Window," *Quality Progress,* Milwaukee, WI: American Society for Quality Control, June, 1987.

Scherkenbach, William W., *The Deming Route to Quality and Productivity,* Rockville, MD: CEE Press, 1986.

———, *Deming's Road to Continual Improvement,* Knoxville, TN: SPC Press, 1991.

Shewhart, Walter A., *The Economic Control of Quality of Manufactured Product,* Princeton, NJ: D. Van Nostrand Company, 1931. Reprinted by American Society for Quality Control, 1980.

Shewhart, Walter A. and W. E. Deming, *Statistical Methods from the Viewpoint of Quality Control,* Washington, D.C.: Department of Agriculture, 1939.

Taguchi, Genichi, *Introduction to Quality Engineering,* White Plains, NY: Asia Productivity Organization, 1986.

Taylor, Frederick W., *The Principles of Scientific Management,* Easton, PA: Hive Publishing Company, 1985.

Tukey, John W., *Exploratory Data Analysis,* Reading, MA: Addison-Wesley, 1977.

United States Department of Defense, *Military Standard 105D. Sampling Procedures and Tables for Inspection by Attributes* (MIL-STD-105D), Washington, D.C.: U.S. Government Printing Office, 1963.

Wheeler, D. J. and D. S. Chambers, *Understanding Statistical Process Control,* Second Edition, Knoxville, TN: SPC Press, 1992.

Whitney, John O., *The Trust Factor: Liberating Profits and Restoring Corporate Vitality,* New York: McGraw-Hill, 1993.

Index